MODERN
EMBROIDERY

MODERN EMBROIDERY

35 stylish and contemporary hand-sewn designs

laura strutt

CICO BOOKS

LONDON NEW YORK

For Wolf and Raven—welcome to the pack, Elkie Raven.

Published in 2019 by CICO Books
An imprint of Ryland Peters & Small Ltd
20–21 Jockey's Fields, London WC1R 4BW
341 E 116th St, New York, NY 10029

www.rylandpeters.com

10 9 8 7 6 5 4 3 2 1

Text © Laura Strutt 2019
Design, illustration, and photography © CICO
Books 2019

A CIP catalog record for this book is available from
the Library of Congress and the British Library.

ISBN: 978-1-78249-602-1

Printed in China

Editor: Sarah Hoggett
Designer: Alison Fenton
Photographer: James Gardiner
Stylists: Nel Haynes and Clare Macdonald
Illustrator: Stephen Dew

Art director: Sally Powell
Production controller: Mai-Ling Collyer
Publishing manager: Penny Craig
Publisher: Cindy Richards

contents

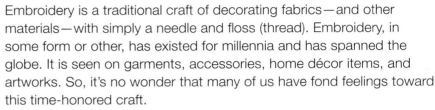

introduction

Embroidery is a traditional craft of decorating fabrics—and other materials—with simply a needle and floss (thread). Embroidery, in some form or other, has existed for millennia and has spanned the globe. It is seen on garments, accessories, home décor items, and artworks. So, it's no wonder that many of us have fond feelings toward this time-honored craft.

The first piece of embroidery that I came into contact with was a fairytale countryside cottage scene (shown left), complete with winding path, blooming English country flowers, and even a happy prancing puppy! It was created by my maternal grandfather, John Herbert Styles, and still takes pride of place in our family home. As much today as when I was a child, I love looking at the intricate design, the combination of colorful threads and stitching that makes this simple scene come alive.

Embroidery is a creative pastime that, for the most part, requires very few supplies, and with a little time and practice the creative possibilities begin to grow and grow. It has enjoyed many reincarnations and is currently gaining in popularity for the wide range of projects and styles that can be created. Modern makers are championing the craft to create highly personalized artworks, customize garments and accessories, and even share pop culture references.

The collection of makes in this book draws from the traditional concepts of rendering designs onto fabrics. I've also embraced modern color combinations and contemporary motifs to create an upbeat collection that will not only be fun to stitch but will also inspire to you create your own unique designs.

Making the projects for this book was a real joy: the process of working solely with my hands to create designs, pictures, and motifs with just a needle and thread is incredibly satisfying for the soul! What's more, this slow stitching craft is a very keen departure from the high-tech, ultra-busy schedules many of us face, making hand embroidery a fabulous crafty antidote for hectic modern lives!

Happy stitching!

Laura

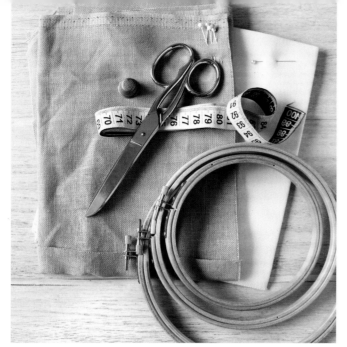

before you begin

Embroidery is a hugely creative and satisfying pastime. Not only will you be able to try out a number of stitches and techniques—often in the same project—but you will also be able to work on something utterly unique. Many of the projects are easily portable, so you'll find yourself taking them with you to work on them whenever you get the chance!

Hints & Tips

• The majority of the makes in this collection are stitched in an embroidery hoop. A hoop is one of the easiest ways to hold the fabric at an even tension, allowing you to work neatly across the surface. Hoops are also relatively inexpensive and extremely lightweight, helping to make the project both easy to handle and portable. Larger-scale designs can be secured in an embroidery frame; there the work is stitched at the ends to the end bars of the frame before being rolled up to create tension.

• In addition to hoops and frames, many stitchers find that using a stand—either a large floor stand with a frame or a small lap stand for hoops—is a great way to support the work. Not only will this give you two hands to stitch and manipulate the threads with, but you will often find that it improves your posture as you work; it's all too easy to hunch over designs, particularly more complex ones.

• If you're adding embroidery to a fabric that has some stretch, such as jersey, you can always use a stabilizer on the wrong side of the fabric to give it some additional support.

• Threading the needle might sound like a very straightforward part of embroidery, but when you're using stranded cottons be sure to check if the design requires you to work with the full number of strands or if you need to separate some out. Aim to work with lengths approximately the length from the tip of your finger to your elbow, as longer lengths are likely to tangle and knot.

• It might not seem like it—especially if you prick your finger or thumb—but the point of embroidery needles gets dull after continued use. This can mean that it takes more effort to work the stitches, which can cause damage to both the fibers of the threads and the fabric. Avoid any unnecessary struggle and damage by replacing your needle after approximately eight hours of use.

• Some designs take a considerable number of hours to complete, so make sure you're sitting comfortably and are not hunched over your work. Natural light is ideal for embroidery; however, working in a well-lit room is great, too!

• Take a tip from the embroiderers of fine fabrics and wash your hands frequently when working with delicate or light-colored fabrics. The natural oils from our skin or any lotions, moisturizers, or make-up can be easily transferred to the fabrics and stitches, causing stains.

• If you plan to leave an embroidery project for a while before completing it, consider removing it from the hoop to prevent the fabric—especially the more delicate ones—from becoming permanently distorted. Slip the work into a clean cloth tote bag or box to prevent damage from dust or moths.

embroidery equipment and supplies

Essentials

Embroidery requires only a few readily available supplies, so you'll quickly be able to get up and running on your next creative project.

Needles

Embroidery or crewel needles have a medium-sized eye in an elongated shape; the shaft of the needle is often slightly thinner than the eye and the tip is nice and sharp, making them ideal for piercing through fabrics to work the stitches. Embroidery needles come in a range of sizes from 1 to 12; 1 is the largest and 12 is the smallest.

You can buy needles in packs that contain a variety of sizes, and these are usually the best option for beginners. The more embroidery you do and the more experience you get of working on different fabrics and with different flosses (threads), the easier you will find it to select the correct needle for your project. Here are some quick tips to help you pick the correct needle size:

• You should be able to draw the needle through the fabric easily and the floss (thread) should follow, including the section at the eye of the needle where the floss is doubled over.
• Flosses should glide easily through the fabrics via the small hole created by the needle. If you feel as though you are really tugging the floss through the fabric, you may need to increase the size of the needle. Alternatively, if you can see a hole in the fabric where the floss has emerged, consider using a smaller needle.
• You may feel or even hear a slight noise as the needle penetrates the fabric. This should be more noticeable where the fabric is held at tension and not from the needle being forced through. If there is a lot of resistance, or the surface of the fabric is becoming warped and pulled, this may be a sign to switch up to a larger needle.

Fabrics

There are almost limitless styles of fabrics that can be used for embroidery! It is most common to work on a woven fabric (rather than a knitted fabric, like jersey, which has more stretch, making it harder to create uniform stitches—see Hints & Tips box, left.) Woven fabrics include cottons, linens, and blended fibers, which are available in a wide range of colors, patterns, and designs. If you're a beginner, you might find lighter-colored fabrics easier to work on, as it is easier to see the stitches as they are being worked against a lighter background.

Floss (thread)

Embroidery flosses are relatively inexpensive and are available in a wide range of colors, so you may find that you have a bright stash of supplies in no time! The most common embroidery floss is "stranded floss," which comprises six strands loosely twisted together. They can be made in a number of different fibers—cotton, silk, linen, or rayon—and are sold in skeins with paper bands listing the brand, color, and fiber information.

Floss bobbins

These are small plastic or card shapes for the floss (thread) to be wound round. Transferring the floss to bobbins will prevent tangles when you come to select and cut lengths for use. Write the shade number of the floss and even the brand on the top of the bobbin, so that you can restock quickly and easily when you run out.

Hoops

There are lots of different styles and sizes of hoops. Mostly they come with two parts that fit snugly together, with the fabric sandwiched in between. Hoops are made wood, plastic, flexible rubbery plastic, or a combination of plastic and metal. A 6-in. (15-cm) hoop is a good medium-sized hoop to start with.

Thread conditioners/beeswax

Although it's not a necessity, many stitchers love using thread conditioners or beeswax to treat the floss prior to stitching. Simply draw the strands across the surface of the conditioner or beeswax; this will leave a very slight coating on the fibers, which will give less resistance when stitching and can help prevent the flosses from tangling or getting frayed.

Frames and stands

As mentioned in Hints & Tips on page 8, these are not essential, but many embroiderers swear by them for comfort while stitching. They hold the frame or hoop steady and can be positioned so that you can work with both hands.

Pens and pencils

There is a wide range of pens and tools for transferring motifs onto the fabric. The most common are fabric pencils, which can be washed off after use. Water-erasable pens allow you to mark out the design and once the stitching is complete the ink can be carefully washed away. Many come in a range of colors, enabling you to pick a shade that will be visible on your chosen fabric. Be sure to test on a small part of the fabric, to ensure that the marks can be removed without leaving a trace!

Scissors

Small, sharp-bladed embroidery scissors are ideal; these will allow you to cut thread lengths and snip away thread ends. You will also need fabric scissors for cutting larger pieces of fabric and pinking shears to prevent fraying.

Thimble

Some stitchers like to slip a thimble on to protect their fingertips when working with thicker fabrics or on larger projects.

Additional supplies

While these items are not essential for embroidery, there are a few handy supplies that you might like to collect together for the finishing or customizing stages of your projects.

Sewing needle and cotton thread

A general-purpose sewing needle is useful for sewing the back of pieces for the finishing of wall art. It is also useful in the making-up stages of other projects. A selection of sewing threads in neutral colors will be handy, too!

Pins

Used to hold fabrics together for sewing in the making-up stages, pins are also useful for holding templates on the surface the fabric when transferring motifs.

Tape measure

This is handy for checking measurements of fabrics and also for helping you to find the center of a piece.

Interfacings

These are available in a range of styles, weights, and colors. Many are fusible and are used to finish the backing of the work or for fusing elements together.

Fray Check

This adhesive is used sparingly along the raw edges of fabrics, cords, and ribbons. Once it has dried, it will help to bond the fibers so that they don't fray (see page 15).

High-tack glue

Specialty glues that can be used for bonding fabrics, plastics, and papers are brilliant for the finishing stages of many projects, particularly if they dry clear.

Embellishments

Buttons, beads, ribbon, ric-rac, and pom-pom trims are often the perfect additions for embellishing and customizing your makes.

Floss storage

Having a box with a lid is a great way to keep your flosses in neat order. It will keep them handy and also prevent them from becoming dusty and dirty. You may find that you can repurpose a vintage biscuit tin, or even a lunchbox! Alternatively, you can buy storage cases made of clear plastic that allow you to stack the wound floss bobbins in separate compartments for easy access.

chapter 1

WALL ART

wall art basics

What better way to show off your embroidery skills than to hang your projects on the wall for all to see? You could, of course, display them in a conventional photo or picture frame, but I like to use the hoop I stitched my design in as the "frame." The fact that it's a standard piece of sewing equipment seems particularly appropriate!

I tend to back my wall art projects with felt. Not only is it very easy to work with, because it doesn't fray, but it can be easily manipulated into place and secured with glue. Alternatively you can sew the felt in place using blanket stitch. Do check that the felt is neatly trimmed, so that it's not visible around the sides of the hoop.

As the felt won't be seen, it's common to pick a neutral shade for the backing, but of course you can select any color you like. Double check that really bright or dark colors don't show through the embroidery fabric from the front.

Most of the wall art projects on pages 16-37 are sewn, framed, and backed in the same way, so just follow the instructions below. Any variations from this basic method are detailed in the individual project instructions.

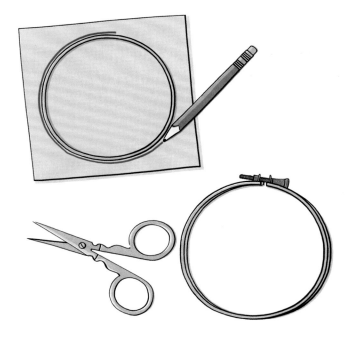

1 First, prepare the felt you'll use to back the piece and hide the reverse of the stitching. Place the inner part of the embroidery hoop on the felt and draw around the outer edge with a fabric transfer pen or pencil. Neatly cut out the shape and set it aside.

2 Using pinking shears, trim the raw edges of fabric you're using for the embroidery to prevent it from fraying. Secure the fabric in the embroidery hoop (see page 118) to create a neat, taut stitching surface.

3 Transfer your embroidery motif centrally onto the fabric (see page 117). Following the stitch guide for your chosen project, work the design in the corresponding colors and stitches.

TIP

Keep the screw fastenings of the hoop at the top of the design, so that you can thread ribbon or cord through them to hang the finished work.

4 Once the design is stitched, work a row of gathering stitches around the outer edge of the fabric, using a sewing needle and cotton thread. Draw the thread up tightly to pull the excess fabric neatly over to the back of the hoop, gathering it firmly, and knot to secure.

TIP

You may prefer to add two rounds of gathering stitches—particularly for square or oval frames. This can help to draw the fabrics in much more neatly around the shape of the frame than a single round of stitches.

TIP

High-tack glue is incredibly sticky, although most brands dry clear. Apply it sparingly so as not to create clumps of dried glue on the finished piece.

5 Apply a small amount of high-tack glue around the inside edge of the hoop and press the backing felt on top to cover the back of the embroidery. Allow the glue to dry completely.

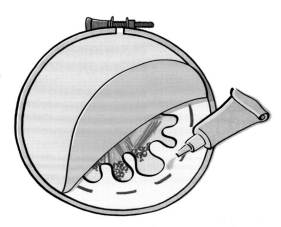

6 Attach a hanging ribbon, cord, or leather thong to the screws at the top of the hoops if required.

Fray Check

Fray Check is a handy product that many embroiderers keep in their supplies kit. If you aren't backing your project with felt, as above (for example, Floating Cloud, page 30), you might like to add some Fray Check to the fabric. This is a quick-drying liquid sealant that, when applied to the edges of the fabrics, will hold and secure the fibers and prevent them from fraying. It can also be used to secure the ends of trimmings and ribbons. Use it sparingly and always check on a scrap or discrete section first to make sure that it doesn't alter the color of the fabrics.

color wheel

Made with only French knots, this striking design is easy to master, even for beginners. Tonal shades are selected to create a dramatic color-wheel effect that will add real impact to your interiors.

The template for the color wheel is just a rough guide for where the colors should be worked; if you stray outside the lines with each color, the blend of shades and tones will be much more organic than if you work directly along the given lines.

YOU WILL NEED:

Natural-colored linen blend fabric (55% linen, 45% cotton), 10-in. (25-cm) square

Neutral-colored felt, 10-in. (25-cm) square

Embroidery flosses (threads)—one skein of each, all six strands used—in the following shades:
  Anchor 2 (White)
  Anchor 6 (Peach)
  Anchor 10 (Coral)
  Anchor 11 (Mid Coral)
  Anchor 13 (Dark Coral)
  Anchor 24 (Mid Pink)
  Anchor 35 (Dark Melon)
  Anchor 48 (Very Light Dusty Rose)
  Anchor 50 (Pale Geranium)
  Anchor 54 (Geranium)
  Anchor 90 (Light Grape)
  Anchor 92 (Violet)
  Anchor 100 (Dark Violet)
  Anchor 109 (Dark Lavender)
  Anchor 111 (Very Dark Lavender)
  Anchor 128 (Very Light Baby Blue)

Anchor 145 (Mid Delft Blue)
Anchor 186 (Mid Seagreen)
Anchor 188 (Very Dark Seagreen)
Anchor 242 (Forest Green)
Anchor 244 (Dark Forest Green)
Anchor 292 (Very Light Golden Yellow)
Anchor 295 (Light Straw)
Anchor 298 (Deep Canary)
Anchor 303 (Light Tangerine)
Anchor 304 (Mid Tangerine)
Anchor 316 (Tangerine)
Anchor 342 (Light Lavender)
Anchor 851 (Very Dark Gray Green)
Anchor 975 (Very Very Light Blue)
Anchor 979 (Very Dark Baby Blue)
Anchor 1043 (Very Light Pistachio Green)
Anchor 1066 (Very Dark Turquoise)
Anchor 1092 (Light Seagreen)

Leather thong, 12 in. (30 cm) long

Small wooden bead

Fabric scissors, pinking shears, and embroidery scissors

Motif and stitch guide on page 17

Embroidery hoop, 6¼ in. (16 cm)

Pencil or tailor's chalk

Embroidery needle

Thread conditioner (optional)

High-tack glue

FINISHED MEASUREMENTS

6¼ in. (16 cm) in diameter

EMBROIDERY STITCHES USED

French knots (see page 114)

STITCHING AND ASSEMBLY

1 Follow the step-by-step instructions on pages 14–15.

2 When you've backed the piece with felt, thread the leather thong through the fastening at the top of the hoop and thread on the small wooden bead before knotting the thong to make a hanging loop.

Follow the step-by-step instructions on pages 14–15.

TIP

Be sure to take the needle back through the fabric slightly past the point where it came up from when making the French knots. This helps prevent the knot from being pulled right back through the fabric, which can damage the weave of the cloth.

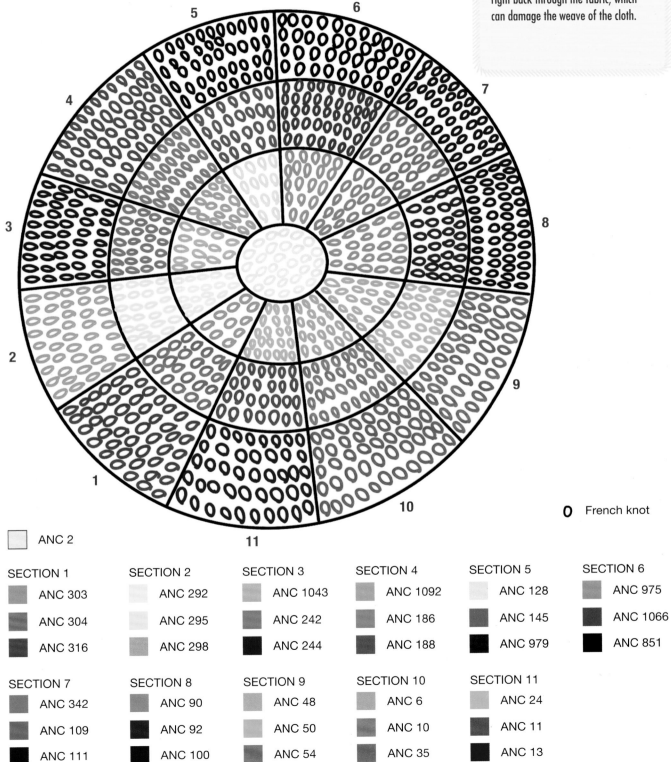

O French knot

ANC 2

SECTION 1	SECTION 2	SECTION 3	SECTION 4	SECTION 5	SECTION 6
ANC 303	ANC 292	ANC 1043	ANC 1092	ANC 128	ANC 975
ANC 304	ANC 295	ANC 242	ANC 186	ANC 145	ANC 1066
ANC 316	ANC 298	ANC 244	ANC 188	ANC 979	ANC 851

SECTION 7	SECTION 8	SECTION 9	SECTION 10	SECTION 11
ANC 342	ANC 90	ANC 48	ANC 6	ANC 24
ANC 109	ANC 92	ANC 50	ANC 10	ANC 11
ANC 111	ANC 100	ANC 54	ANC 35	ANC 13

Add some New-Age style to your décor with this trio of crystals wall art. Worked in satin stitch featuring ombré shades, you can customize it by using your own favorite color palette: simply choose four shades of the same color along with white, light gray, and dark gray floss (thread) for outlining.

colorful crystals

YOU WILL NEED
Cream linen blend fabric (55% linen, 45% cotton), one 10-in. (25-cm) and two 8-in. (20-cm) squares

Neutral-colored felt, one 10-in. (25-cm) and two 8-in. (20-cm) squares

Embroidery flosses (threads)—one skein of each, all six strands used—in the following shades:

For the purple crystals
Anchor 2 (White)
Anchor 90 (Light Grape)
Anchor 92 (Violet)
Anchor 94 (Mid Plum)
Anchor 100 (Dark Grape)
Anchor 235 (Dark Steel Gray)
Anchor 400 (Pewter Gray)

For the blue-green crystals
Anchor 2 (White)
Anchor 185 (Light Aquamarine)
Anchor 187 (Dark Seagreen)
Anchor 188 (Very Dark Seagreen)
Anchor 235 (Dark Steel Gray)
Anchor 400 (Pewter Gray)
Anchor 1092 (Light Seagreen)

For the pink crystals
Anchor 2 (White)
Anchor 60 (Mid Mauve)
Anchor 62 (Cyclamen Pink)
Anchor 65 (Cranberry)
Anchor 77 (Mauve)
Anchor 235 (Dark Steel Gray)
Anchor 400 (Pewter Gray)

Ribbon in toning colors to hang if required—approx. 12 in. (30 cm) per motif

Motifs and stitch guides on page 19

Fabric scissors, pinking shears, and embroidery scissors

Embroidery hoops, one 5 in. (12 cm) and two 4 in. (10 cm)

Embroidery needle

Thread conditioner (optional)

Sewing needle and cotton thread

High-tack glue

FINISHED MEASUREMENTS
5 in. (12 cm) and 4 in. (10 cm) in diameter

EMBROIDERY STITCHES USED
French knots (see page 114)
Satin stitch (see page 115)
Straight stitch (see page 116)

STITCHING AND ASSEMBLY

Follow the step-by-step instructions on pages 14–15. This design is worked largely in satin stitch; maintain an even tension to create a neat finished piece.

0   French knot

   Satin stitch

/   Straight stitch

 ANC 100

 ANC 94

ANC 92

ANC 90

ANC 2

ANC 235

ANC 400

ANC 188

ANC 187

ANC 185

ANC 1092

ANC 2

ANC 235

ANC 400

ANC 65

ANC 77

ANC 62

ANC 60

ANC 2

ANC 235

ANC 400

Use the larger hoop for this embroidery.

prickly pictures

Don't worry if you don't have green fingers—you can simply sew your own plants that will stay in bloom the whole year round! This collection of miniature frames is quick to stitch and makes a fun focal point for a small space. Mini frames are available in craft stores and are usually a very simple design with only two parts, making the process of trimming and securing the work quick and easy.

YOU WILL NEED

Cream linen blend fabric (55% linen, 45% cotton), 12-in. (30-cm) square

Embroidery flosses (threads)—one skein of each, all six strands used—in the following shades:
  DMC 163 (Mid Celadon Green)
  DMC 350 (Mid Coral)
  DMC 502 (Blue Green)
  DMC 602 (Mid Cranberry)
  DMC 822 (Light Beige Gray)
  DMC 3011 (Dark Khaki Green
  DMC 3012 (Mid Khaki Green)
  DMC 3013 (Light Khaki Green)
  DMC 3722 (Mid Shell Pink)

Grosgrain ribbon, blue, 65 in. (165 cm), ⅜ in. (1 cm) wide

Five miniature craft frames

Motifs and stitch guide on page 21

Fabric scissors, pinking shears, and embroidery scissors

Embroidery hoop, 7½ in. (19 cm)

Embroidery needle

Thread conditioner (optional)

High-tack glue

Fray Check

FINISHED MEASUREMENTS

Assorted sizes, approx. 1¾ in. (4.5 cm)

EMBROIDERY STITCHES USED

Backstitch (see page 112)
Cross stitch (see page 113)
French knots (see page 114)
Satin stitch (see page 115)
Straight stitch (see page 116)
Weave stitch (see page 116)

STITCHING AND ASSEMBLY

1 Follow steps 1–3 on page 14, making sure you leave enough space around each one when you transfer the motifs onto the linen fabric.

2 Remove the fabric from the hoop and trim each design to about ⅛ in. (3–4 mm) smaller than the outer edge of the frame. Apply a small amount of Fray Check to the edges to help bond the fibers. Allow to dry, as per the manufacturer's instructions.

3 Place each motif in turn on the back part of the relevant frame. Apply a small amount of high-tack glue around the front of the frame and press it in place, sandwiching the design in place.

4 Cut the ribbon into one 16½-in. (41-cm), two 13¾-in. (35-cm), and two 10½-in. (27-cm) lengths. Secure through the upper loop of the frame to finish.

TIP

These motifs can also be stitched next to each other to create a grouped design for displaying in a single frame.

 DMC 602

DMC 350

DMC 3012

DMC 3013

DMC 3011

DMC 822

DMC 502

DMC 3722

DMC 163

 Weave stitch

0 French knot

X Cross stitch

| Backstitch

Z Satin stitch

/ Straight stitch

botanical filled letter

This embroidered letter makes a great personalized piece of home décor or a truly special gift. The outline of the letter is carefully filled with a range of botanical-inspired stitches. It's a great way to showcase your growing embroidery skills, too!

A whole alphabet appears on page 122, so you can personalize this piece to your own requirements. To fill the shape of the letter fully, add in extra woven roses or leaf stitches to neatly fill out the outline shape of the letter.

YOU WILL NEED

Neutral-colored felt, 12-in. (30-cm) square

Dark neutral-colored felt for backing, 10-in. (25-cm) square

Embroidery flosses (threads)—one skein of each, all six strands used—in the following shades:
DMC 315 (Mid Dark Antique Mauve)
DMC 316 (Mid Antique Mauve)
DMC 501 (Dark Blue Green)
DMC 562 (Mid Jade)
DMC 822 (Light Beige Gray)
DMC 961 (Dark Dusty Rose)
DMC 3011 (Dark Khaki Green)
DMC 3013 (Light Khaki Green)
DMC 3687 (Mauve)

Motif and stitch guide below.

Fabric scissors and embroidery scissors

Flexi embroidery hoop, 7-in. (18-cm) square

Embroidery needle

Thread conditioner (optional)

Sewing needle and cotton thread

High-tack glue

FINISHED MEASUREMENTS

7 in. (18 cm) square

EMBROIDERY STITCHES USED

Backstitch (see page 112)
French knots (see page 114)
Herringbone leaf stitch (see page 114)
Satin stitch (see page 115)
Straight stitch (see page 116)
Woven rose (see page 116)

TIP

This design has been worked on neutral-colored felt to make the colors of the botanical-themed stitches pop. You can pick a brighter shade if you prefer something a little more coordinated.

STITCHING AND ASSEMBLY

Follow the step-by-step instructions on pages 14–15.

DMC 822
DMC 315
DMC 316
DMC 961
DMC 3687
DMC 3013
DMC 3011
DMC 501
DMC 562

Backstitch
Satin stitch
French knot
Herringbone leaf stitch
Woven rose
Straight stitch

alphabet sampler

Traditionally stitch samplers were a means to practice different stitches and letterforms, and this colorful example is a modern take on a classic design. Using a font inspired by vintage tattoos and a rainbow color palette, this wall hanging will be sure to brighten your interiors!

It's displayed on a homemade hanging bar, the instructions for which are given below—but if you don't want to make your own, you can buy one ready made from art and craft stores or online.

YOU WILL NEED

Linen blend fabric (55% linen, 45% cotton) in a neutral color, 15 x 11½ in. (38 x 29 cm)

Cork fabric for backing, 8 x 11 in. (20 x 28 cm)

Fusible web, 8 x 11 in. (20 x 28 cm)

Embroidery flosses (threads):

Two skeins, all six strands used, in the following shade:
  Anchor 430 (Black)

One skein, all six strands used, in the following shades:
  Anchor 9 (Light Coral)
  Anchor 10 (Coral)
  Anchor 11 (Mid Coral)
  Anchor 13 (Very Dark Coral)
  Anchor 24 (Mid Pink)
  Anchor 46 (Bright Red)
  Anchor 48 (Very Light Dusty Rose)
  Anchor 54 (Geranium)
  Anchor 90 (Light Grape)
  Anchor 109 (Dark Lavender)
  Anchor 111 (Very Dark Lavender)
  Anchor 145 (Mid Delft Blue)
  Anchor 170 (Very Dark Peacock Blue)
  Anchor 188 (Mid Aquamarine)
  Anchor 211 (Bright Green)
  Anchor 242 (Forest Green)
  Anchor 244 (Dark Forest Green)
  Anchor 295 (Light Straw)
  Anchor 298 (Deep Canary)
  Anchor 301 (Pale Yellow)
  Anchor 303 (Light Tangerine)
  Anchor 316 (Tangerine)
  Anchor 338 (Light Terracotta)
  Anchor 342 (Light Lavender)
  Anchor 851 (Very Dark Gray Green)
  Anchor 1066 (Very Dark Turquoise)

Wooden batten, 35½ x ¼ in. (90 cm x 5 mm)

Four pairs of strong, thin magnets, ¼ in. (5 mm) in diameter

Leather hanging thong, 12 in. (30 cm)

Motif and stitch guide on page 26

Embroidery hoop, 5 in. (12.5 cm)

Embroidery needle

Embroidery scissors

Thread conditioner (optional)

Pressing cloth and iron

Saw

Sandpaper

Wood stain or varnish and paintbrush (optional)

High-tack glue

FINISHED MEASUREMENTS

8¼ x 11¾ in. (21 x 30 cm)

EMBROIDERY STITCHES USED

Backstitch (see page 112)
French knots (see page 114)
Straight stitch (see page 116)

TIP

This project uses small amounts of lots of colors of floss (threads) to create a rainbow effect across the alphabet. Alternatively, use threads that you have or pick a single color or ombré tones of one shade.

STITCHING AND ASSEMBLY

1 Follow steps 1–3 on page 14.

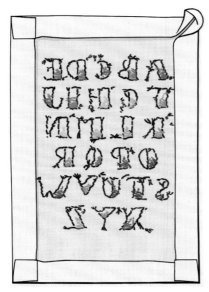

2 Once the design is stitched, neatly knot and trim all the thread ends. Cover with a pressing cloth and press flat on the reverse. Fold over 1 in. (2.5cm) to the wrong side around the whole of the embroidered panel, making neat miter folds at the corners, and press again.

3 Place the embroidered panel wrong side up. Center the fusible web on top, with the cork backing fabric right side up on top of that. Cover with a pressing cloth and press to fuse the layers together.

4 Using the saw, cut the wood into four 8¼-in. (21-cm) lengths. Sand all surfaces. Apply wood stain or varnish, if you wish.

5 Place a magnet 1 in. (2.5 cm) in from each end on one piece of wood and fix it in place with high-tack glue. Position the other half of each magnet on the corresponding part of the next piece of wood and glue to secure; this creates the top of the frame. Make the bottom of the frame in the same way.

6 Knot each end of the length of leather thong and sandwich it in between the two upper parts of the frame to create a hanging loop. Secure the sampler by placing a piece of wood at the front and back of the work; the magnets will hold it in place.

■	ANC 430

ROW 1

■	ANC 46
■	ANC 13
■	ANC 10
■	ANC 11
■	ANC 54

ROW 2

■	ANC 9
■	ANC 24
■	ANC 48
■	ANC 338
■	ANC 316

ROW 3

■	ANC 303
■	ANC 298
■	ANC 295
■	ANC 301

ROW 4

■	ANC 211
■	ANC 244
■	ANC 188
■	ANC 242

ROW 5

■	ANC 170
■	ANC 851
■	ANC 1066
■	ANC 145
■	ANC 111

ROW 6

■	ANC 109
■	ANC 90
■	ANC 342

This chart is reproduced at 50%. To make it full size, you will need to enlarge it by 200% on a photocopier.

0	French knot
/	Backstitch
//	Satin stitch

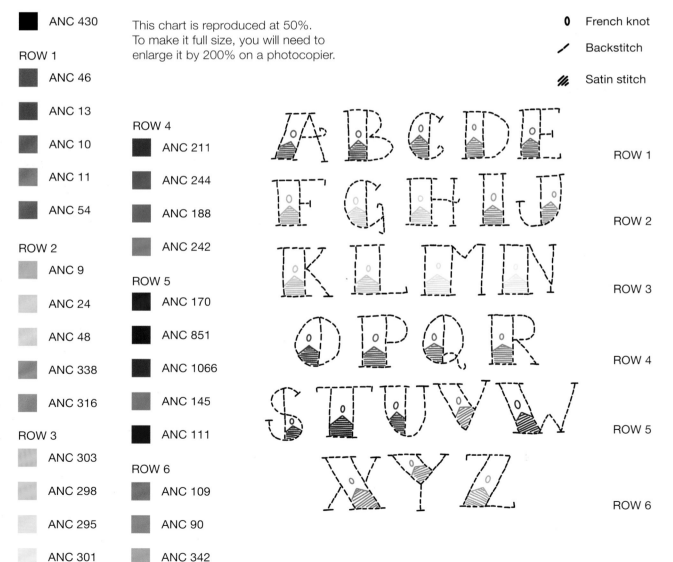

ROW 1
ROW 2
ROW 3
ROW 4
ROW 5
ROW 6

double hoop wreath

Combining two embroidery hoops to create a centered stitching space is a really great way to branch out with your embroidery. Here the double hoops have been used to display a festive wreath, complete with sparkles, candy canes, and bows!

YOU WILL NEED

Linen blend fabric (55% linen, 45% cotton) in a neutral color, 20-in. (50-cm) square

Neutral-colored felt, 20-in. (50-cm) square

Embroidery flosses (threads):

Two skeins, all six strands used, in the following shades:
  Anchor 211 (Bright Green)
  Anchor 877 (Dark Celadon Green)

One skein, all six strands used, in the following shades:
  Anchor 2 (White)
  Anchor 13 (Very Dark Coral Red)
  Anchor 209 (Light Emerald Green)
  Anchor 310 (Light Brown)
  Anchor 403 (Black)

Selection of sequins

Red velvet ribbon, 39 in. (100 cm), 1 in. (2.5 cm) wide

20-in. (50-cm) length of cord

Motif and stitch guide on page 29

Fabric scissors, pinking shears, and embroidery scissors

Embroidery hoops, 9 in. (23 cm) and 5 in. (12.5 cm)

Embroidery needle

Thread conditioner (optional)

High-tack glue

Sewing needle and cotton thread

FINISHED MEASUREMENTS

9 in. (23 cm) in diameter

EMBROIDERY STITCHES USED

Backstitch (see page 112)
Long and short stitch worked at random (see page 115)
Satin stitch (see page 115)

STITCHING AND ASSEMBLY

1 Trim the raw edges of the linen fabric with pinking shears to it from prevent fraying. Find the center of the fabric and secure the smaller hoop in place. Turn the fabric over; this will leave the inner part of the smaller embroidery hoop visible on the surface.

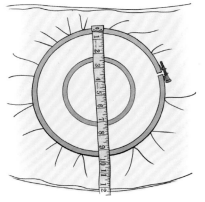

TIP

Take your time securing and positioning the two hoops; not only do you need the hoops to be centered for neatness, you also need to have an even tension across the fabric that will be stitched.

2 Position the larger hoop around the smaller hoop. Take time to ensure that the hoop is centered; you can double check by measuring the distance between the hoops at intervals around the circle. Carefully fasten the second hoop in place to create a taut stitching surface.

3 Transfer the wreath motif on page 29 onto the linen between the two hoops. Following the stitch guide, work the design in the corresponding colors and stitches. Secure some sequins in place using the sewing needle and cotton thread.

4 Gather the outer fabric, following step 4 on page 15.

5 Make small snips in the fabric inside the smaller hoop, cutting from the center to just inside the edge of the hoop; this will form a series of long, thin, triangular pieces of fabric.

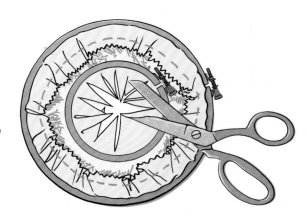

TIP

When sewing the excess fabric to reveal the hole at the center you might find that you get neater results by working twice around the wreath, as this will allow you to gradually draw the fabrics together neatly.

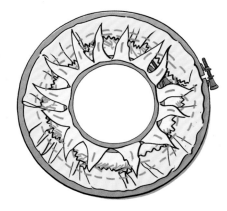

6 Using a sewing needle and cotton thread, stitch through the points of the cut fabric triangles and then draw them back toward the outer ring and secure them on the gathered fabric. This will expose the hole at the center of the wreath. Take care not to stitch right through to the embroidered section!

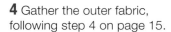

7 Tie the ribbon into a large bow with equal-length tails and, using the sewing needle and cotton thread, stitch it to the upper part of the wreath. If you wish, you can secure the ribbon tails to the sides of the wreath.

8 Center the completed wreath on top of the backing felt, draw around the outer ring, and cut out. Apply high-tack glue around the outer hoop and also around the inside of the smaller central hoop, then place the circle of felt on top. The felt backing will temporarily cover the hole at the center.

9 Once the glue has dried, make a small snip in the center of the felt inside the smaller inner hoop and neatly trim away the felt to reveal the hole at the center. Thread the length of cord through the upper screw and knot it to make a hanging loop.

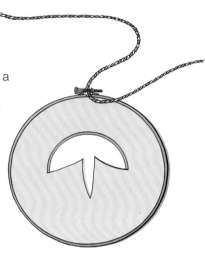

This chart is reproduced at 50%. To make it full size, you will need to enlarge it by 200% on a photocopier.

■	ANC 403
░	ANC 2
▓	ANC 13
▓	ANC 310
▒	ANC 209
▓	ANC 211
■	ANC 877

⁄	Backstitch
⦚	Satin stitch
⫽⫽	Long and short stitch worked at random

floating cloud

Switching out a thick fabric for an almost translucent material—such as netting or organza—can create visually stunning pieces. The cloud motif is worked on a net background to give the illusion of it floating in the sky!

STITCHING AND ASSEMBLY

1 Follow step 2 on page 14, filling in the outline of the cloud motif with French knots in white floss (thread).

2 Once the design is stitched, remove it from the hoop and set aside. Place the rainbow ribbon centrally over the lower part of the outer hoop, fold over ⅜ in. (1 cm) to the back of the hoop, and glue it in place.

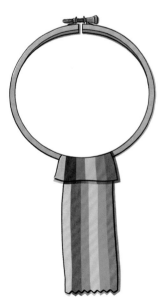

TIP

Netting is very fine and you may find that it doesn't stay taut in the embroidery hoop. To create a more snug fit for stitching, try wrapping a length of cotton fabric around the inner hoop before you secure the netting to give it more grip.

TIP

Lightweight fabrics such as netting and organza are very easy to rip when stitching. You may find that supporting the back of the fabric with one hand while working the French knots helps to prevent damaging the fabric.

YOU WILL NEED:

White netting, 6-in. (15-cm) square

Embroidery floss (thread)—two skeins, all six strands used—in the following shade:
  Anchor 2 (White)

Mini pom-pom trim, 18 in. (45.5 cm)

Rainbow ribbon, 4½ in. (11.5 cm), 1½ in. (4 cm) wide

Motif and stitch guide on page 31

Fabric scissors, pinking shears, and embroidery scissors

Embroidery hoop, 5 in. (12.5 cm)

Embroidery needle

Thread conditioner (optional)

High-tack glue

Fray Check

FINISHED MEASUREMENT

5 in. (12.5 cm) in diameter

EMBROIDERY STITCHES USED

French knots (see page 114)

3 Once the glue has dried, reposition the embroidered netting in the frame and draw it taut before fastening the hoop. Trim the fabric close to the back of the hoop and apply a coat of Fray Check to the raw edges around the hoop back to secure.

4 Once dry, position the mini pom-pom trim in place and attach it to the outer edge of the frame with dabs of high-tack glue.

ANC 2

0 French knot

Whether you're creating a special keepsake for yourself or to give as gift, this personalized motif makes a unique piece of wall art. This design is worked in a flexi embroidery hoop, which has a rubbery, flexible outer ring that not only secures the cloth while you work but also acts as a focal point on the finished piece.

love letters

YOU WILL NEED

Cream linen blend fabric (55% linen, 45% cotton), 10-in. (25-cm) square

Neutral-colored felt, 10-in. (25-cm) square

Embroidery flosses (threads)—one skein of each, all six strands used—in the following shades:
DMC 502 (Blue Green)
DMC 950 (Light Desert Sand)
DMC 961 (Dark Dusky Rose)
DMC 979 (Very Dark Baby Blue)
DMC 3012 (Mid Khaki Green)
DMC 3041 (Mid Antique Violet)

Blue gingham ribbon to hang if required—approx. 12 in. (30 cm), 3⁄8 in. (1 cm) wide

Motif and stitch guide, below

Fabric scissors, pinking shears, and embroidery scissors

Pencil or tailor's chalk

Flexi embroidery hoop, 6½ in. (17 cm)

Embroidery needle

Thread conditioner (optional)

Sewing needle and cotton thread

High-tack glue

FINISHED MEASUREMENTS

6½ in. (17 cm) in diameter

EMBROIDERY STITCHES USED

Backstitch (see page 112)
French knots (see page 114)
Herringbone leaf stitch (see page 114)
Satin stitch (see page 115)
Straight stitch (see page 116)
Woven rose (see page 116)

STITCHING AND ASSEMBLY

Follow the step-by-step instructions on pages 14–15.
To change the letters and numbers, use the templates on page 121.

DMC 979

DMC 961

DMC 3041

DMC 950

DMC 3012

DMC 502

| Backstitch

≋ Satin stitch

0 French knot

Herringbone leaf stitch

Woven rose

↓ | ✳ Straight stitch

doodle family portrait

Whether you create this for your own family or to give as a gift, a custom portrait will be sure to become a talking point. The simple doodle-style characters here are based on my own little family.

YOU WILL NEED

Linen blend fabric (55% linen, 45% cotton) in a neutral color, 11 x 6 in. (28 x 15 cm)

Neutral-colored felt, 11 x 6 in. (28 x 15 cm)

Embroidery flosses (threads)—one skein of each, all six strands used—in the following shades:
  Anchor 9 (Light Coral)
  Anchor 10 (Coral)
  Anchor 46 (Bright Red)
  Anchor 98 (Violet)
  Anchor 242 (Forest Green)
  Anchor 298 (Deep Canary)

Anchor 338 (Light Terracotta)
Anchor 349 (Golden Brown)
Anchor 351 (Dark Mahogany)
Anchor 400 (Pewter Gray)
Anchor 403 (Black)
Anchor 831 (Very Light Drab Brown)
Anchor 936 (Very Dark Desert Sand)
Anchor 1066 (Very Dark Turquoise)
Anchor 1094 (Very Light Cranberry)

Motif and stitch guide below

Embroidery hoop, oval, 5 x 9 in. (12.5 x 23 cm)

Fabric scissors, pinking shears, and embroidery scissors

Embroidery needle

Thread conditioner (optional)

Sewing needle and cotton thread

High-tack glue

FINISHED MEASUREMENTS

5 x 9 in. (12.5 x 23 cm)

EMBROIDERY STITCHES USED

Backstitch (see page 112)
French knots (see page 114)
Straight stitch (see page 116)

STITCHING AND ASSEMBLY

Follow the step-by-step instructions on pages 14-15.

ANC 9	ANC 1094	ANC 98	ANC 298	– – –	Backstitch
ANC 400	ANC 10	ANC 349	ANC 351		
ANC 46	ANC 242	ANC 1066	ANC 936	0	French knots
ANC 403	ANC 831	ANC 338		/ /	Straight stitch

TIP

Each likeness can be customized to fit your loved ones. You can change the gender, skin tones, hair styles, and hair colors—and even switch out the dog for a cat!

constellations

Worked in very simple French knots and straight stitches in white thread on inky-black batik fabric, this makes a striking piece of wall art.

TIP

Create a more personal design by working the constellation for your own star sign.

YOU WILL NEED

Black batik fabric, 10-in. (25-cm) square

Neutral-colored felt, 10-in. (25-cm) square

Embroidery floss (thread)—one skein in the following shade:
  Anchor 275 (Off White)—use all six strands for French knots and three strands for straight stitches

Hot pink grosgrain ribbon, 90 in. (230 cm), ⅜ in. (1 cm) wide

Motif and stitch guide, below

Fabric scissors, pinking shears, and embroidery scissors

Embroidery hoop, 6½ in. (16.5 cm)

Embroidery needle

Thread conditioner (optional)

High-tack glue

FINISHED MEASUREMENTS

6½ in. (16.5 cm) in diameter

EMBROIDERY STITCHES USED

French knots (see page 114
Straight stitch (see page 116)
Straight stitch star (see page 116)

STITCHING AND ASSEMBLY

1 Follow steps 1–3 on page 14, using six strands of floss (thread) for the French knots and the straight stitch stars, and three for the straight stitches. Once the design is complete, remove it from the hoop and set it aside.

2 Glue the end of the pink grosgrain ribbon to the tip of the outer hoop and begin to wrap it around, overlapping to cover the surface, using dabs of glue to secure it as you work. (High-tack glue should dry clear, but be sure to add the glue only to the inside of the hoop so that it won't be visible on the finished piece.) Tuck both raw ends in to neaten and set aside to dry fully.

3 Once the glue has set and the ribbon is firmly attached, place the embroidered fabric back in the hoop and secure it in place. Complete the project by following steps 4–6 on page 15.

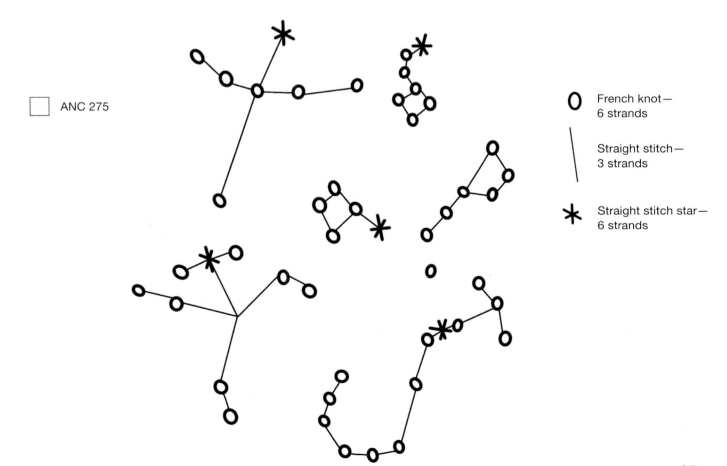

ANC 275

○ French knot—6 strands

╱ Straight stitch—3 strands

✳ Straight stitch star—6 strands

chapter 2
HOME

home sweet home key keeper

Our homes are our castles and hand-making a colorful key fob is not only a pretty addition to your keychain, but also helps you to find your keys in the recesses of your purse! Embroidered on felt, this accessory is soft, with fray-resistant edges.

YOU WILL NEED

White felt, 6-in. (15-cm) square

Fusible web, 3½ x 4 in. (9 x 10 cm)

Print cotton fabric, 3½ x 4 in. (9 x 10 cm)

Embroidery flosses (threads)—one skein of each, all six strands used—in the following shades:
  DMC 150 (Very Dark Dusty Rose)
  DMC 158 (Medium Dark Cornflower Blue)
  DMC 502 (Blue Green)
  DMC 950 (Light Desert Sand)
  DMC 962 (Mid Dusty Rose)
  DMC 972 (Deep Canary)
  DMC 3041 (Mid Antique Violet)
  DMC 3678 (Teal)
  DMC 3722 (Mid Shell Pink)
  DMC 3863 (Mid Mocha Beige)

Grosgrain ribbons: blue, 6 in. (15 cm), ½ in. (1.5 cm) wide, and coral, 6 in. (15 cm), ⅜ in. (1 cm) wide

Small split ring keyring

Motif and stitch guide on page 42

Fabric scissors, pinking shears, and embroidery scissors

Embroidery hoop, 4½ in. (11 cm)

Embroidery needle

Thread conditioner (optional)

Sewing needle and cotton thread

Pressing cloth and iron

FINISHED MEASUREMENTS

Approx. 2⅛ x 2½ in. (5.5 x 6.5 cm)

EMBROIDERY STITCHES USED

Backstitch (see page 112)
French knots (see page 114)
Long and short stitch (see page 115)
Running stitch (see page 115)
Satin stitch (see page 115)

1 Secure the felt in the embroidery hoop (see page 118) to create a neat, taut stitching surface.

2 Transfer the cottage motif on page 42 centrally onto the felt (see page 117). Following the stitch guide on page 42, work the design in the corresponding colors and stitches.

TIP

If you are using air-erasable or water-erasable pens to mark out the motif, be sure to test on a small section at the edge first.

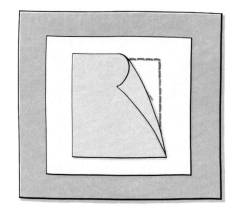

3 Remove the felt from the hoop and place it right side down on a pressing cloth. Center the fusible web over the back of the embroidered motif.

TIP

Why not personalize this key ring by drawing and embroidering your own home, or make one for a friend who has just moved house.

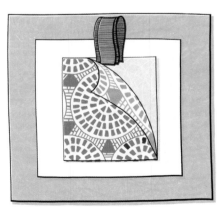

4 Lay the narrow piece of ribbon on top of the wider one, fold them in half, and position them centrally on the top edge. Place the print cotton on top, right side up. Following the manufacturer's instructions fuse the layers together, sandwiching the ribbon loop between the layers.

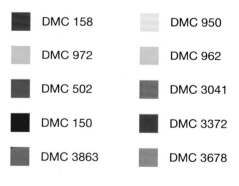

5 Using pinking shears and making sure the embroidered design is centered, trim the piece to 2⅛ x 2½ in. (5.5 x 6.5 cm).

6 Add a split ring to the ribbon loop to finish.

■ DMC 158	■ DMC 950
■ DMC 972	■ DMC 962
■ DMC 502	■ DMC 3041
■ DMC 150	■ DMC 3372
■ DMC 3863	■ DMC 3678

0	French knot
/	Backstitch
‖‖	Long and short stitch
/-	Running stitch
⌇	Satin stitch

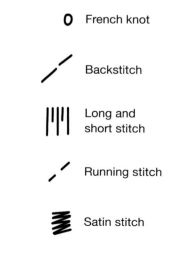

sweet-scented sachet

Give your clothes some TLC by adding a sweet-scented lavender bag to your closet. Not only will it give your garments a delicate fragrance, but it will help to ward off those pesky moths, too! This floral motif, worked in bullion stitch and French knots, plays up the vintage charm.

1 Using the pinking shears, trim the raw edges of the linen fabric to prevent it from fraying. Secure it in the embroidery hoop (see page 118) to create a neat, taut stitching surface.

2 Transfer the lavender motif on page 45 centrally onto the fabric (see page 117). Following the stitch guide, work the design in the corresponding colors and stitches.

3 Once the design is complete, remove it from the hoop and trim it to 3½ x 4½ in. (9 x 11 cm). Trim the solid cotton to 3½ x 2 in. (9 x 5 cm) and the print cotton to 3½ x 5½ in. (9 x 14 cm). Put the print cotton to one side.

4 With right sides together, place the solid cotton strip along the bottom of the embroidered linen panel and pin in place. Using a straight machine or hand stitch and taking a ⅜-in. (1-cm) seam allowance, stitch the two together to create a single panel. Press the seam open.

YOU WILL NEED

Linen blend fabric (55% linen, 45% cotton) in a neutral color, 6-in. (15-cm) square

Solid cotton fabric, 3½ x 2 in. (9 x 5 cm)

Print cotton fabric, 3½ x 5½ in. (9 x 14 cm)

Embroidery flosses (threads)—one skein of each, all six strands used—in the following shades:
  Anchor 110 (Very Dark Blue Violet)
  Anchor 111 (Very Dark Lavender)
  Anchor 779 (Dark Gray Green)
  Anchor 1209 (Variegated Violet)
  Anchor 1216 (Variegated Khaki Green)

Gold grosgrain ribbon, 7½ in. (19 cm), ⅜ in. (1 cm) wide

Small piece of batting (wadding) or fabric scraps

Dried lavender

Oblong button, ⅝ in. (1.5 cm) long

Motif and stitch guide on page XX

Fabric scissors, pinking shears, and embroidery scissors

Embroidery hoop, 4½ in. (11 cm)

Embroidery needle

Thread conditioner (optional)

Pins

Sewing needle and cotton thread

Sewing machine (optional)

Pressing cloth and iron

FINISHED MEASUREMENTS
2¾ x 4¾ in. (7 x 12 cm)

EMBROIDERY STITCHES USED
Bullion stitch (see page 112)
French knots (see page 114)
Stem stitch (see page 115)
Straight stitch (see page 116)

TIP

Ensure that you have the correct number of wraps per stitch for bullion stitch and French knots in order to create uniform stitches.

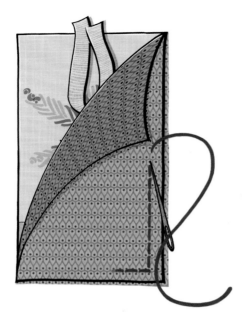

5 Fold the ribbon in half to make a small loop, then center it on the upper edge of the embroidery with the loop pointing inward. Pin the print cotton on top, right sides together, sandwiching the ribbon loop in between. Using a straight machine or hand stitch and taking a ⅜-in. (1-cm) seam allowance, stitch all around, leaving a 1½-in. (4-cm) gap along the bottom edge.

6 Clip the corners of the seam allowance neatly and turn the bag right side out through the gap. Cover with a pressing cloth and press lightly, ensuring that the seam allowances of the gap in the seam are pressed inward.

7 Insert a small piece of batting (wadding) or some fabric scraps into the pouch to lightly stuff it. Fill with dried lavender. Using a sewing needle and cotton thread, slipstitch the gap in the seam closed. Place the small button at the base of the ribbon loop and sew it securely in place.

TIP

Use the trimmed-off edges of your other embroidery makes to lightly stuff the lavender bag.

ANC 1209	
ANC 110	
ANC 111	
ANC 779	
ANC 1216	

Straight stitch

Bullion stitch

French knot

Stem stitch

Add a personal touch to your table settings with this pair of botanical-inspired napkins. Work in either a coral or aqua floss (thread) to add a flash of contrast to the monstera leaf motifs. These are surprisingly quick to make, so are brilliant last-minute housewarming gifts.

botanical napkins

YOU WILL NEED
Cotton napkins

Embroidery flosses (threads)—one skein of each, all six strands used—in the following shades:
Leaf shades:
  Anchor 211 (Bright Green)
  Anchor 215 (Mid Pistachio Green)
Contrast shades:
  Anchor 33 (Mid Melon)
  Anchor 186 (Mid Seagreen)

Motif and stitch guide on page 47

Embroidery hoop, 4½ in. (11.5 cm)

Embroidery needle

Embroidery scissors

Thread conditioner (optional)

Pressing cloth and iron

FINISHED MEASUREMENTS
Motif: approx. 4 in. (10 cm) square

EMBROIDERY STITCHES USED
Backstitch (see page 112)
French knots (see page 114)

1 Secure the napkin in the embroidery hoop (see page 118) to create a neat, taut stitching surface, making sure that the hoop is positioned toward a corner.

TIP

These designs can be worked on store-bought napkins or you can make your own from fabrics to suit your décor.

2 Transfer the monstera leaf motif on the right to the napkin (see page 117). Following the stitch guide, work the design in the corresponding colors and stitches.

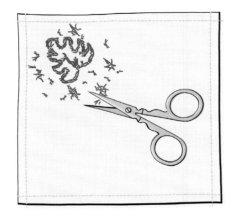

3 Once the design is complete, remove the napkin from the frame and trim the thread ends neatly. Place under a pressing cloth and press on the reverse to finish.

4 Repeat steps 1–3 to make the second napkin in the pair, working in the alternative colorway for the contrast accents.

ANC 33	
ANC 186	
ANC 211	
ANC 215	

0 French knot

/ Backstitch

rainbow mandala tote bag

As we all ditch plastic in favor of environmentally friendly options, this project is the perfect opportunity to add a flash of personality to your shopping bags. Worked in a range of different stitches that give you the chance to practice your skills, this bold mandala motif is a great way to brighten up an everyday canvas tote bag.

YOU WILL NEED

Tote bag, 15 x 16½ in. (38 x 42 cm)

Heavyweight fusible interfacing, 10-in. (25-cm) square

Embroidery flosses (threads)—one skein of each, all six strands used—in the following shades:
  DMC 164 (Light Forest Green)
  DMC 208 (Very Dark Lavender)
  DMC 321 (Red)
  DMC 518 (Light Wedgwood Blue)
  DMC 741 (Mid Tangerine)
  DMC 743 (Mid Yellow)
  DMC 962 (Mid Dusty Rose)

Motif and stitch guide on page 49

Embroidery hoop, 9 in. (22 cm)

Embroidery needle

Embroidery scissors

Thread conditioner (optional)

Pressing cloth and iron

FINISHED MEASUREMENTS

Bag: 15 x 16½ in. (38 x 42 cm)
Mandala motif: 8 in. (20 cm) in diameter

EMBROIDERY STITCHES USED

Chain stitch (see page 113)
Cross stitch (see page 113)
French knots (see page 114)
Lazy daisy stitch (see page 113)
Running stitch (see page 115)

TIP

The heavier weight of the fabric for a tote bag means that you will probably find transfer paper the best method for transferring the motif onto the fabric for stitching.

1 Transfer the mandala motif below centrally onto the tote bag (see page 117). Secure it in the embroidery hoop (see page 118) to create a neat, taut stitching surface. Following the stitch guide, work the design in the corresponding colors and stitches.

2 Remove the work from the hoop and place the stitching right side down on a pressing cloth.

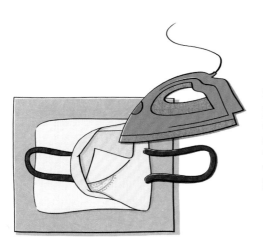

3 On the inside of the tote bag, place the square of interfacing adhesive side down over the back of the stitches so that it covers all the embroidery. Fuse in place following the manufacturer's instructions.

TIP

Applying interfacing to the inside of the bag will cover the back of the stitches and prevent them from getting snagged or damaged when the bag is in use.

This chart is reproduced at 50%. To make it full size, you will need to enlarge it by 200% on a photocopier.

DMC 321
DMC 741
DMC 743
DMC 164
DMC 518
DMC 962
DMC 208

O French knot

X Cross stitch

∂ Chain stitch

I Running stitch

∂ Lazy daisy

hanging heart decorations

Inspired by traditional folk-style embroidery, these hanging heart decorations make use of the bold contrast of red and white. Create your own to add a handmade touch to holiday celebrations or even wedding parties.

YOU WILL NEED

Red felt, two 10-in. (25-cm) squares

White felt, two 10-in. (25-cm) squares

Embroidery flosses (thread)—one skein of each, all six strands used—in the following shades:
  Anchor 2 (White)
  Anchor 46 (Bright Red)

Toy stuffing

Cord for hanging loops, 20 in. (50 cm), (makes two loops)

White button, 2 in. (25 mm) in diameter

Motif and stitch guide on page 52

Fabric and embroidery scissors

Embroidery hoop, 6 in. (15 cm)

Embroidery needle

Thread conditioner (optional)

Pins

FINISHED MEASUREMENTS

Each decoration is approx.
4½ x 4 in. (12 x 10 cm)

EMBROIDERY STITCHES USED

French knots (see page 114)
Lazy daisy stitch (see page 113)
Running stitch (see page 115)
Stem stitch (see page 115)
Straight stitch (see page 116)

1 Set aside one piece of felt in each color. Secure one of the remaining pieces of felt in turn in the embroidery hoop (see page 118) to create a neat, taut stitching surface. Transfer the heart motif on page 52 centrally onto the felt. Following the stitch guide, work the design in the corresponding color and stitches—white floss (thread) on red felt or vice versa. Do not sew the running stitch outline yet.

2 Remove the work from the hoop. Place the stitching right side up on the remaining piece of felt in the same color and pin the layers together.

TIP

You can work the embroidered panel twice for each decoration to make them double sided—be sure to align them neatly before you sew them up.

3 Cut the cord in half, then fold one length in half to make a loop. Tie the loose ends in a small knot, then slip the knotted ends between the two layers of felt at the center top of the heart, so that the cord is sandwiched inside.

4 Place the decorative button on top and secure in place with a few stitches, stitching through both layers of felt and the cord.

5 Work a line of running stitch around the outer edge of the stitched heart motif to secure the embroidered front to the plain back of the decoration. Once two-thirds of the seam is complete, begin to fill the heart with toy stuffing, continuing until the decoration is lightly padded. Complete the seam and knot discretely to finish.

6 Using fabric scissors, carefully cut around the outline of the heart, about ¼ in. (6 mm) beyond the running stitches.

7 Make the second heart decoration in the same way, using the opposite colorway.

ANC 46 on white felt or ANC 2 on red felt

| Straight stitch
¦ Running stitch
Stem stitch
Lazy daisy
French knot

Stow your treasures away in a stylish stitched storage box. A single shade of floss (thread) against a bold cotton background makes a striking finished piece. This design features a simple floral motif and repeated shapes inspired by traditional Scandinavian folk art.

tulip treasure box

1 Using the pinking shears, trim the raw edges of the mustard cotton fabric to prevent it from fraying. Secure it in the embroidery hoop (see page 118) to create a neat, taut stitching surface.

2 Transfer the tulip motif on page 54 centrally onto the fabric (see page 117). Following the stitch guide, work the design in the corresponding stitches.

3 Remove the work from the hoop. Center the backing board of the box frame or photo frame over the back of the embroidery.

YOU WILL NEED

Mustard cotton fabric, 10-in. (25-cm) square

Heavyweight fusible interfacing, 4-in. (10-cm) square

Embroidery floss (thread)—three skeins, all six strands used—in the following shade:
  Anchor 2 (White)

Wooden photo frame or box frame, 6 x 6 x 4 in. (15 x 15 x 10 cm)

Motif and stitch guide on page 54

Fabric scissors, pinking shears, and embroidery scissors

Embroidery hoop, 9 in. (22 cm)

Embroidery needle

Thread conditioner (optional)

Sewing needle and cotton thread

High-tack glue

Pressing cloth and iron

FINISHED MEASUREMENTS

Box frame: 6 x 6 x 4 in (15 x 15 x 10 cm)
Embroidery: 4 x 4 in. (10 x 10 cm)

EMBROIDERY STITCHES USED

Backstitch (see page 112)
French knots (see page 114)
Satin stitch (see page 115)
Weave stitch (see page 116)

TIP

This embroidery is mounted in a customizable jewelry box, available from craft stores. The same technique can be used to secure the work in a traditional picture frame to display on the wall.

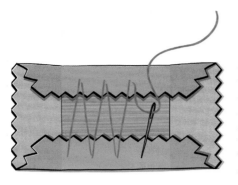

4 Fold the top and bottom edges of the fabric in over the backing board and temporarily secure the edges with a few small dabs of glue. Using the sewing needle and cotton thread, work a long lacing stitch to draw the fabric tight over the frame. Knot securely.

TIP

Lacing stitch is used to draw the fabric around the central part of the frame. Maintain an even tension to ensure that the fabric remains smooth and isn't pulled out of shape.

5 Fold the side edges in over the portion of the frame and secure with lacing stitch in the same way. Once the fabric is taut around the backing board, secure with a knot.

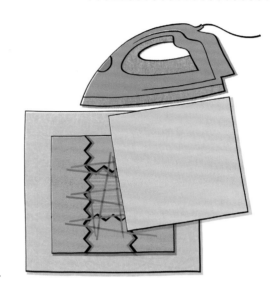

6 Place the embroidery right side down. Place the square of fusible interfacing over the backing board and cover with a pressing cloth. Fuse in place, following the manufacturer's instructions.

7 Insert the embroidery into the box lid or the frame.

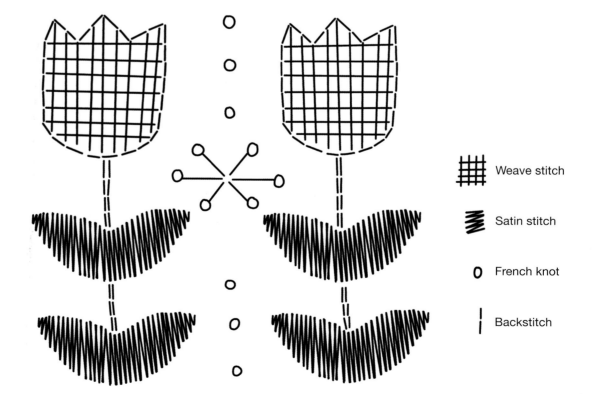

■ ANC 2

▦ Weave stitch

≋ Satin stitch

0 French knot

| Backstitch

Accessorize your sewing kit in style with this custom-made needle book and pincushion set. Combining simple stitches onto felt, this is a quick and easy make that beginners will love!

needle book and pincushion

YOU WILL NEED

For the needle book

Lilac felt, 12-in. (30-cm) (square

White felt, 8-in. (20-cm) square

Solid cotton for lining, 8-in. (20-cm) square

Fusible web, 8-in. (20-cm) square

Embroidery flosses (threads)—one skein of each, all six strands used—in the following shades:
   Anchor 185 (Very Light Seagreen)
   Anchor 187 (Dark Seagreen)
   Anchor 401 (Very Light Ash Gray)
   Anchor 831 (Very Light Drab Brown)

Ribbon with tape-measure motif, 6 in. (15 cm), ⅜ in. (1 cm) wide

Motif and stitch guide on page 58

For the pincushion

Jar with removable lid (Mason/Kilner style)

Solid cotton, 4-in. (10-cm) square

Small scrap of white felt

Embroidery floss (thread)—one skein, all six strands used—in the following shade:
   Anchor 63 (Mid Cranberry)

Toy filling or kitchen scouring pad

Small button

Fabric scissors, pinking shears, and embroidery scissors

Embroidery hoop, 5 in. (12.5 cm)

Embroidery needle

Thread conditioner (optional)

Sewing needle and cotton thread

High-tack glue

FINISHED MEASUREMENTS

Needle book: 4½ x 7½ in. (11 x 19.5 cm) when open
Pincushion: 2½ in. (6cm) in diameter

EMBROIDERY STITCHES USED

Backstitch (see page 112)
Chain stitch (see page 113)
French knots (see page 114)
Satin stitch (see page 115)

FOR THE NEEDLE BOOK

1 On the lilac felt, mark out an area measuring 4½ x 7½ in. (11 x 19.5 cm). Transfer the cotton reel motif on page 58 onto what will be the front of the book (see page 117).

2 Secure the felt in the embroidery hoop (see page 118) to create a neat, taut stitching surface. Following the stitch guide, work the design in the corresponding colors and stitches.

3 Once the design is complete, remove the felt from the hoop and neatly trim it along the lines marked in step 1.

4 Trim the ribbon to 5 in. (12.5 cm) and glue it across the bottom of the needle book cover, ensuring that a small portion extends over to the back of the book and a small portion is left to be folded to the inside.

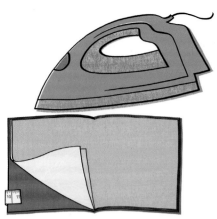

5 Trim the solid lining cotton and the fusible web to 4½ x 7½ in. (11 x 19.5 cm). Place the embroidered felt wrong side up, with the fusible web on top and the lining fabric right side up on top of that. Tuck the remaining edge of ribbon inside the layers. Following the manufacturer's instructions, fuse the layers together.

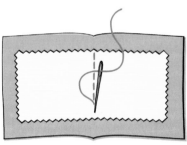

6 Using pinking shears, trim the white felt to 3½ x 6½ in. (9 x 16.5 cm). Fold the felt sheet in half and position it in the center of the needle book. Secure in place with a line of running stitches along the spine of the needle book, then knot the thread to finish.

TIP

You can add more pages to your needle book to accommodate more sewing supplies by simply cutting additional sheets of felt, layering them neatly, and securing them along the spine of the needle book.

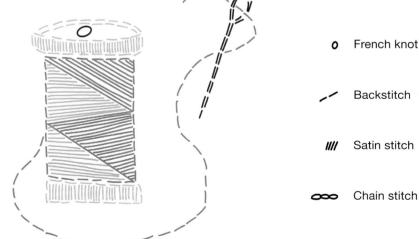

ANC 187

ANC 185

ANC 401

ANC 831

o French knot

— Backstitch

//// Satin stitch

∞ Chain stitch

FOR THE PINCUSHION

1 Measure the circumference of the jar and, using pinking shears, cut a piece of lilac felt ⅜ in. (1 cm) longer than the circumference by ⅝ in. (1.5 cm) wide.

2 Mark a central line down the strip of felt if needed, and work a length of chain stitches across the strip in mid cranberry floss (thread). Knot the threads securely.

3 Place the strip around the center of the jar and secure it in place with high-tack glue.

4 Remove the lid from the jar and separate the lid sections. Using pinking shears, cut out a circle of fabric that is 2 in. (5 cm) larger all around than the lid and set it aside.

5 Make the pincushion by rolling up a handful of toy filling or trimming the kitchen scouring pad into a dome shape that is slightly smaller than the base of the jar lid.

6 Place the pincushion filling/scouring pad dome in the center of the fabric. With pinking shears, cut a small circle of white felt and place it in the center of the pincushion, with the button on top. Using the sewing needle and cotton thread, sew the button and felt circle to the center of the pincushion, drawing it through the fabric and the pincushion filling. Knot tightly to secure.

TIP

A kitchen sponge/scouring pad makes a great insert for a pincushion. Not only can it be trimmed to the perfect shape, but the abrasive material means it keeps your pins and needles sharp.

7 Using the sewing needle and cotton thread, work a line of gathering stitches (see page 15) around the outer edge of the cotton fabric. Draw up the thread ends to cover the filing and knot securely.

8 Insert the pincushion through the ring of the lid and secure the base of the pincushion to the base of the lid with high-tack glue before screwing the lid in place.

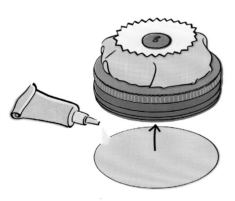

sashiko table mat set

Sashiko—which translates literally as "little stitches" or "little stabs"—is a very traditional Japanese style of embroidery. It is often used to reinforce fabrics, but it is very decorative in its simplicity. Here, the Sashiko-style stitching has been used to customize store-bought placemats.

YOU WILL NEED

Store-bought placemats, 13½ x 16 in. (34.5 x 41 cm)

Motif and stitch guide on page 51

Embroidery flosses (threads)—one skein of each, all six strands used—in the following shades:
  DMC Blanco (white)
  DMC 310 (Black)

Embroidery needle

Embroidery scissors

Thread conditioner (optional)

Thimble (optional)

Pressing cloth and iron

FINISHED MEASUREMENTS

13½ x 16 in. (34.5 x 41 cm)

EMBROIDERY STITCHES USED

Running stitch (see page 115)

TIP

Try to make all your running stitches the same length, to keep the design looking neat and professional.

1 Transfer the Sashiko-inspired motif below onto the placemat (see page 117). Following the stitch guide, work the design in running stitch in the corresponding colors.

2 Once the design is complete, knot the threads at the back of the work and snip the ends to neaten. Place under a pressing cloth and press on the reverse to finish.

This chart is reproduced at 50%. To make it full size, you will need to enlarge it by 200% on a photocopier.

 DMC BLANCO

DMC 310

— — Running stitch

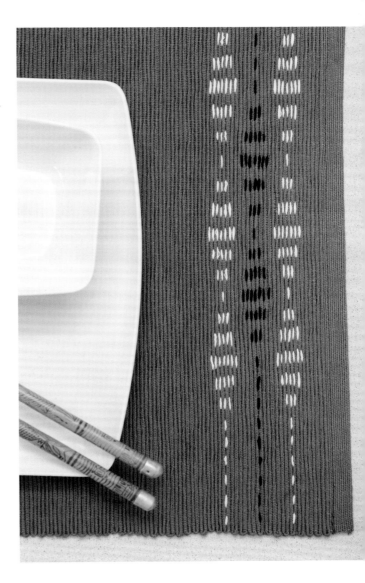

stitch sampler pillow

Samplers are a traditional form of embroidery, allowing you to work on and perfect a number of different styles of stitching in a single project. This design allows you to try your hand at ten different stitching styles in a contemporary color palette before making it up into a cozy pillow (cushion).

YOU WILL NEED:

Low-volume geometric fabric, 15-in. (38-cm) square

Solid cotton fabric, 19 x 42 in. (50 x 105 cm)

Embroidery flosses (threads)—one skein of each, all six strands used—in the following shades:
   Anchor 10 (Coral)
   Anchor 147 (Royal Blue)
   Anchor 297 (Bright Canary)
   Anchor 403 (Black)
   Anchor 877 (Dark Celadon Green)

Pillow form (cushion pad), 14-in. (35.5-cm) square

Motif and stitch guide on page 65

Fabric scissors, pinking shears, and embroidery scissors

Embroidery hoop, 7½ in. (19 cm)

Embroidery needle

Thread conditioner (optional)

Sewing machine (optional)

Sewing needle and cotton thread

Pins

Pressing cloth and iron

FINISHED MEASUREMENTS:

Pillow (cushion): 14-in. (35.5-cm) square
Embroidered panel: 10-in. (25-cm) square

EMBROIDERY STITCHES USED:

Backstitch (see page 112)
Blanket stitch (see page 112)
Chain stitch (see page 113)
Couching (see page 113)
Cross stitch (see page 113)
Fern stitch (see page 113)
French knots (see page 114)
Running stitch (see page 115)
Straight stitch star (see page 116)
Threaded running stitch (see page 115)

NOTE

Low-volume fabric refers to a white, cream, or very light gray fabric with a subtle print—dots, stripes, geometrics, and even text.

1 Using the pinking shears, trim the low-volume fabric neatly. Referring to the motif and stitch guide on page 65, mark out the stitches on the fabric, leaving a 2-in. (5-cm) border around the outside.

2 Secure the fabric in the embroidery hoop to create a neat and taut stitching surface (see page 118).

3 Following the stitch guide on page 65, work the design in the corresponding colors and stitches, repositioning the hoop as necessary.

4 Once the design is stitched, remove it from the hoop. Fold 1¼ in. (3 cm) to the wrong side along each side, cover with a pressing cloth, and press on the reverse. Set aside while you prepare the cover.

5 From the solid cotton, cut three pieces—one measuring 15-in. (38-cm) square for the front of the pillow cover, and two measuring 15 x 10½ in. (38 x 26.5 cm) for the back.

TIP

Using a low-volume geometric fabric as a base for your sampler, as here, not only gives you a guide to work neat stitches but also adds a modern feel to your make.

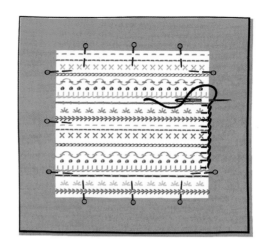

TIP

To keep the blanket stitches around the outer edge of the work a uniform size, mark the two lines of the stitch on the thumb of your hand holding the fabric. When you're holding the work, these lines will clearly show where to insert your needle for each stitch!

6 Place the embroidered panel right side up on the square of solid cotton, ensuring that there is an even border of fabric all around, and pin in place. Using black embroidery floss (thread), work blanket stitch around the embroidered panel to attach it to the solid cotton panel; this will be the front panel.

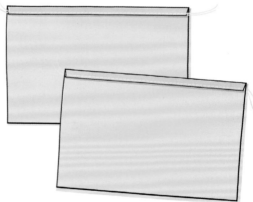

7 On each of the two remaining solid cotton panels, press and fold ⅜ in. (1 cm) to the wrong side along one of the long edges, then fold and press again to create a double-fold hem. Pin and machine stitch or hand sew in place. These are the back panels.

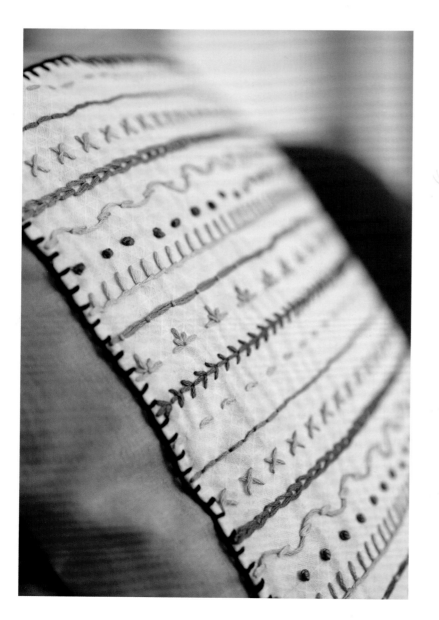

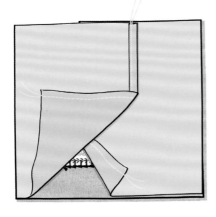

8 With right sides together, line up the raw edges of the two back pieces with the raw edges of the front panel; the edges of the back panels that you hemmed in the previous step will overlap in the center. Pin in place.

9 With a ⅜-in. (1-cm) seam allowance, machine stitch all around the outer edge. Clip the corners and turn right side out. Insert the pillow form (cushion pad).

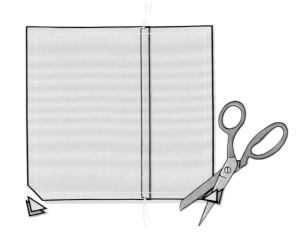

This chart is reproduced at 50%.
To make it full size, you will need to enlarge it by 200% on a photocopier.

ANC 147

ANC 877

ANC 297

ANC 10

— — Running stitch

- - - - Backstitch

✕ Cross stitch

∞ Chain stitch

Threaded running stitch

O French knot

LLL Blanket stitch

Couching

Straight stitch star

Fern stitch

chapter 3
GIFTS

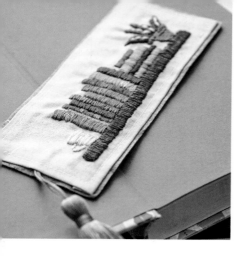

bookworm's pagekeeper

Many of us book lovers adore the sight of a shelf stacked with wonderful new reads—so why not create a custom pagemarker loaded with neatly satin-stitched books? It's teamed with a silky tassel to help you find your place.

YOU WILL NEED

Cotton fabric in a neutral shade, 8-in. (20-cm) square

Felt, 8 x 4 in. (20 x 10 cm)

Fusible web, 8 x 4 in. (20 x 10 cm)

Tassel, 6 in. (15 cm) long

Embroidery flosses (threads)—one skein of each, all six strands used—in the following shades:
  DMC 350 (Mid Coral)
  DMC 602 (Mid Cranberry)
  DMC 632 (Very Dark Desert Sand)
  DMC 700 (Bright Green)
  DMC 959 (Mid Seagreen)
  DMC 972 (Deep Canary)
  DMC 3024 (Very Light Brown Gray)
  DMC 3041 (Mid Antique Violet)
  DMC 3768 (Dark Gray Green)
  DMC 3826 (Golden Brown)
  DMC E677 (Metallic Gold)

Motif and stitch guide on page 69

Fabric scissors, pinking shears, and embroidery scissors

Embroidery hoop, 6 in. (15 cm)

Embroidery needle

Thread conditioner (optional)

Sewing machine (optional)

Pressing cloth and iron

FINISHED MEASUREMENTS

Approx. 6 x 2½ in. (15.5 x 6.5 cm)

EMBROIDERY STITCHES USED

Backstitch (see page 112)
Satin stitch (see page 115

1 Using the pinking shears, trim the raw edges of the cotton fabric to prevent it from fraying. Secure it in the embroidery hoop (see page 118) to create a neat, taut stitching surface.

2 Transfer the bookshelf motif on page 69 centrally onto the fabric (see page 117). Following the stitch guide, work the design in the corresponding colors and stitches.

3 Once the design is complete, remove it from the hoop and neatly trim it to 6½ x 3 in. (16.5 x 7.5 cm), making sure the embroidery is centered. Neatly fold ¼ in. (5 mm) to the wrong side on all sides and press in place.

TIP

Using pinking shears to prepare the cotton fabric before stitching will help prevent frayed fibers from coming loose and getting tangled up in the stitching.

4 Cut the felt to 6½ x 3 in. (16.5 x 7.5 cm) and the fusible web to 6 x 2½ in. (15 x 6 cm). Center the fusible web on top of the felt, with the tassel positioned in the middle of the left-hand short edge and ¾ in. (2 cm) of the tassel's loop sandwiched in between the two layers.

TIP

Placing the work right side down on a pressing cloth (or a fluffy towel) and pressing on the wrong side will help prevent the stitches from being crushed or damaged by the heat of the iron.

5 Place the embroidered panel right side up on top of the fusible web, then carefully flip the whole piece over and cover it with a pressing cloth. Following the manufacturer's instructions, fuse the felt to the wrong side of the embroidered panel.

6 Work a line of straight machine or hand running stitches all around the edge of the embroidered panel to make a border, then trim the felt to ⅛ in. (2–3 mm) larger than the panel.

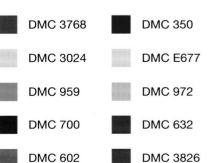

■ DMC 3768		■ DMC 350	
■ DMC 3024		■ DMC E677	
■ DMC 959		■ DMC 972	
■ DMC 700		■ DMC 632	
■ DMC 602		■ DMC 3826	
■ DMC 3041			

 Backstitch   Satin stitch

snowflake gift tag and card

Handmade cards and tags add a truly personal touch to the festive season. These embroidered snowflake designs can be worked on any color of card to add a handmade flair.

YOU WILL NEED

Card blank (or card to cut to size), 4 x 6 in. (10 x 15 cm) when folded

Card for inside card, 3¾ x 5¾ in. (9.5 x 14.5 cm)

Card for tag, 9-in. (22-cm) square

Cord, 10 in. (25 cm) long

Decorative washi tape

Embroidery flosses (threads)—three skeins, all six strands used—in the following shades:
  DMC Blanc (white)
  DMC E677 (Metallic Gold)

Motifs, and stitch guide on page 72

Template on page 123

Tracing paper

Pencil

Embroidery needle

Embroidery scissors

Paper scissors

Thread conditioner (optional)

High-tack glue or double-sided tape

Hole punch

FINISHED MEASUREMENTS

Card: 4 x 6 in. (10 x 15 cm) when folded
Tag: 2¼ x 4 in. (5.5 x 10 cm)

EMBROIDERY STITCHES USED

Backstitch (see page 112)

MAKING THE CARD

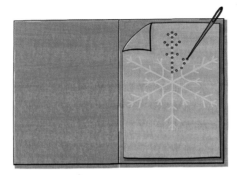

1 Trace the snowflake motif on page 72, then place the tracing paper on the front of the card, and go over the motif with a needle to make small, evenly spaced holes where the stitches are going to be.

2 Inserting your needle through the holes and referring to the motif and stitch guide on page 72, backstitch over the lines of the design.

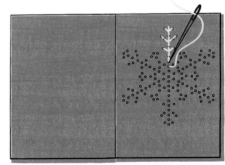

3 Once the design is complete, trim the threads neatly and apply a strip of decorative washi tape across the bottom of the card, folding the end of the tape inside the card to secure.

TIP

Making the holes ahead of sewing the design might sound time consuming, but it's a great way to ensure that the stitches are neat and in the correct position.

4 Cut a piece of card measuring 3¾ x 5¾ in. (9.5 x 14.5 cm). Apply small dabs of high-tack glue or double-sided tape to one side and place it over the back of the work to conceal the stitching.

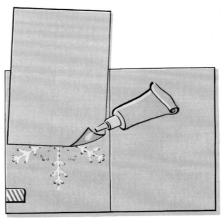

MAKING THE GIFT TAG

1 Using the template on page 123, cut out the gift tag from card. Repeat steps 1 and 2 of the card (see page 70) to make marker holes for the stitches. Lightly score the fold line down the center of the tag, taking care not to cut all the way through.

2 Inserting your needle through the holes and referring to the motif and stitch guide below, backstitch over the lines of the design.

TIP

Sewing through paper and card is quite different from sewing on fabric. Work slowly to be sure you don't crease or rip the surface as you work.

3 Once the design is complete, trim the threads neatly and apply a strip of decorative washi tape to the upper portion of the tag, folding the end of the tape inside to secure.

4 Fold the tag along the score line and press with your fingers to get a sharp crease to conceal the stitching on the back of the tag. Secure in place with high-tack glue or double-sided tape.

5 Punch a small hole at the center top of the tag and thread the cord through it, knotting it to form a loop.

DMC BLANC

DMC E677

Backstitch

star-space purse

This is a "negative-space" design: it's worked from the outline of the motif outward, leaving a star-shaped space in the center. Here it's been made into a simple zippered purse for everyday appeal.

YOU WILL NEED

Blue chambray, 17-in. (45-cm) square

Orange print cotton for lining, 17-in. (45-cm) square

Embroidery flosses (threads)—one skein of each, all six strands used—in the following shades:
  Anchor 170 (Very Dark Peacock Blue)
  Anchor 189 (Dark Bright Green)
  Anchor 301 (Pale Yellow)
  Anchor 317 (Pewter Gray)
  Anchor 323 (Light Orange Spice)
  Anchor 900 (Dark Burnt Orange)

6¼-in. (16-cm) zipper

Small split ring

Motif and stitch guide on page 75

Fabric scissors, pinking shears, and embroidery scissors

Embroidery hoop, 5 in. (12 cm)

Embroidery needle

Thread conditioner (optional)

Pins

Sewing machine with zipper foot (optional)

Sewing needle and cotton thread

FINISHED MEASUREMENTS

Approx. 4¾ x 6 in. (12 x 15 cm)

EMBROIDERY STITCHES USED

French knots (see page 114)

TIP

Using a thread conditioner or running your thread length on a piece of beeswax (see page 11) can prevent snagging while you work French knots.

1 On the chambray, mark out an area measuring 5 x 6 in. (12.5 x 15 cm); this will be the front of the purse. Secure it in the embroidery hoop (see page 118) to create a neat, taut stitching surface.

TIP

To work in random colors, use a shorter length of thread than normal, work a few French knots around the motif, and fasten off. Then work in a different color for a few more knots, and continue in this manner to fill the spaces.

2 Transfer the star motif on page 75 centrally onto the marked area of the fabric (see page 117). Work the design in French knots, using the colors randomly, and try to keep the stitches that outline the star shape in straight lines to get a crisp, clean-edged "negative shape."

3 Once the design is complete, cut out the marked 5 x 6-in. (12.5 x 15-cm) section. From the remaining chambray, cut a second 5 x 6-in. (12.5 x 15-cm) piece. Cut two 5 x 6-in. (12.5 x 15-cm) pieces and a 2 x 4-in. (5 x 10-cm) strip from the orange print cotton and set them aside.

4 Place one piece of orange print lining fabric right side up, with the zipper right side up on top, aligning the edges. Place the embroidered panel right side down on top and pin the layers together, creating a "sandwich" with the zipper in the middle.

5 Fit a zipper foot to your sewing machine and straight stitch between the edge of your zipper "sandwich" and the zipper teeth, stitching close to the zipper teeth.

6 Bring the lining and chambray fabric to the same side, so they're wrong sides together.

7 Repeat steps 4 and 5 to make another zipper "sandwich" on the other side of the zipper. Topstitch along both edges of the zipper; this will prevent the fabric from getting caught in the zipper teeth. Open the zipper partway. (If you forget to do this, you won't be able to turn your purse right side out.)

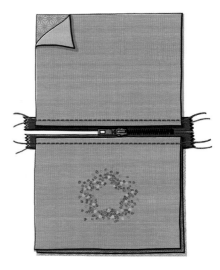

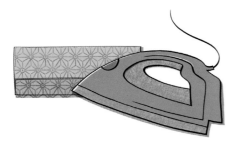

8 Fold the 2 x 4-in. (5 x 10-cm) orange cotton strip in half, wrong sides together, and press. Open it out, fold the long edges into the center crease, and press again; fold along the center crease and topstitch down each long edge. Fold the strip in half to form a loop and stitch across the short edge to secure.

9 Open out the fabrics so that the two lining pieces are right sides together and the two chambray pieces are right sides together. Pin in place. Place the loop in between the two outer pieces in the center of the short edge nearest the zipper pull, aligning the raw edges, and pin in place. Place two pins about 3 in. (7.5 cm) apart on the bottom edge of the lining fabrics to mark where to start and finish stitching. Taking a ¼-in. (6-mm) seam allowance, stitch all around.

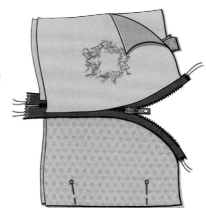

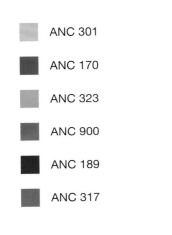

10 Snip off the corners of the seam allowance and turn the purse right side out through the gap. Push the corners out fully. Press the raw edges of the gap to the inside and slipstitch or straight stitch (see page 116) to secure.

11 Push the lining into the purse through the open zipper. Add the split ring to the fabric loop to finish.

ANC 301	
ANC 170	
ANC 323	
ANC 900	
ANC 189	
ANC 317	

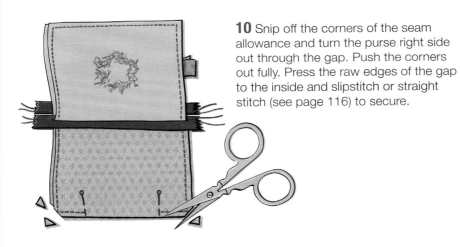

0 French knot

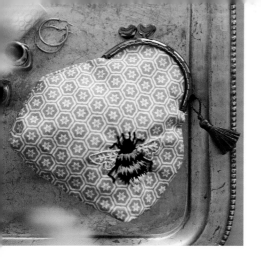

bumblebee purse

This sweet bumblebee motif is quick and fun to stitch and because only a few colors of floss are used, it is really striking. Play up the motif by using a bold honeycomb-print cotton to create a really pretty snap-frame purse.

YOU WILL NEED:

Print cotton, 22-in. (55-cm) square

Solid white cotton for lining, 22-in. (55-cm) square

Snap-frame purse kit—3⅛-in. (8-cm) size used here

Embroidery flosses (threads)—one skein of each, all six strands used—in the following shades:
  Anchor 291 (Dark Lemon)
  Anchor 403 (Black)
  Anchor 926 (Cream)

Motif and stitch guide on page 78

Fabric and embroidery scissors

Embroidery hoop, 5 in. (12.5 cm)

Embroidery needle

Thread conditioner (optional)

Sewing machine

Pins

Sewing needle and cotton thread

Small tassel

Pressing cloth and iron

FINISHED MEASUREMENTS:

Bumblebee motif: 2½ in. (6 cm)

EMBROIDERY STITCHES USED:

Backstitch (see page 112)
Fern stitch (see page 113)
Long and short stitch worked at random (see page 115)
Satin stitch (see page 115)

TIP

If your snap-frame purse kit doesn't have a template included, use the one on page 124 and adapt it to fit, or simply draw around the upper portion of the frame and draw out the base of the purse, being sure to add a ⅜-in. (1-cm) seam allowance all around.

2 Transfer the bumblebee motif on page 72 onto one of the print cotton purse panels (see page 117). Be sure to set it at least 1 in. (2.5 cm) away from the side to avoid it being lost in the seams when you construct the purse. Secure the fabric in the embroidery hoop (see page 118) to create a neat, taut stitching surface. Following the stitch guide, work the design in the corresponding colors and stitches.

3 Once the design is complete, remove it from the hoop and ensure that all the thread ends are neatly trimmed. Cover with a pressing cloth or soft towel and press on the reverse.

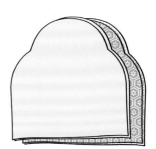

1 Use the template on page 124 or the pattern from the kit (see tip) to mark out the purse pieces on the print cotton and lining fabric. Cut out two pieces from each fabric.

TIP

Although it's more common to embroider on a plain fabric rather than a printed one, sometimes it can really add to the design. If in doubt, draw out your embroidery motif on tracing paper and place it over the fabric to see how well the fabric pattern and the embroidered design work together.

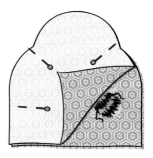

4 Pin the two outer purse pieces right sides together. Repeat with the lining pieces.

5 Machine stitch the two outer purse panels together, taking a ⅜-in. (1-cm) seam allowance. Start at the base of the snap frame and work down the side, across the bottom, and up the second side before finishing at the other end of the snap frame. Repeat with the lining pieces.

6 Create box corners in the outer purse by aligning the side and base seam on the inside, marking a line across ¾ in. (2 cm) from the corner, and sewing along this line to secure. Repeat on opposite corners and snip away the excess fabric. Repeat with the lining.

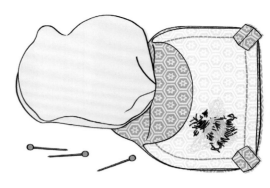

7 Turn the lining right side out. Slide the lining into the purse outer via the upper opening, so that the right sides of the fabrics are together. Align the upper sections and pin in place.

8 Working in two separate seams, join the lining and the outer purse together around the upper portion of the purse, using a straight machine stitch and taking a ⅜-in. (1-cm) seam allowance. Be sure to leave a small gap in one of the seams for turning through.

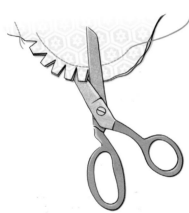

9 Clip small V-shapes in the seam allowance around the curve at the top of the purse. Turn the purse right side out through the gap in the seam. Press neatly, pressing the seam allowance at the gap inward, and then slipstitch the gap closed.

10 Place the upper part of the purse in the snap frame and sew it securely in place to finish. Secure the tassel to the frame.

 ANC 403

ANC 926

ANC 291

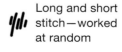 Backstitch

Long and short stitch—worked at random

Satin stitch

Fern stitch

geometric travel card wallet

Stow your everyday essential bank cards or travel pass in a handmade wallet featuring an embroidered geometric motif. Cork fabric is a fabulous alternative to leather and vinyl and makes a great and unusual base for embroidery.

YOU WILL NEED

Cork fabric, 14-in. (35.5-cm) square

Pink print cotton, for lining, 14-in. (35.5-cm) square

Fusible web, 8 x 11 in. (20 x 28 cm)

Embroidery flosses (thread)—one skein of each, all six strands used—in the following shades:
  DMC 312 (Very Dark Baby Blue)
  DMC 602 (Mid Cranberry)
  DMC 743 (Mid Yellow)
  DMC 943 (Mid Aquamarine)
  DMC 959 (Mid Seagreen)
  DMC 972 (Deep Canary)

Template on page 125

Motif and stitch guide on page 81

Fabric and embroidery scissors

Embroidery hoop (optional)

Embroidery needle

Thread conditioner (optional)

Pins

Sewing machine (optional)

Sewing needle and cotton thread

Pressing cloth and iron

FINISHED MEASUREMENTS

6½ x 4½ in. (17 x 11 cm) when open

EMBROIDERY STITCHES USED

Satin stitch (see page 115)

1 Using the template on page 125, mark out the two wallet inserts on the cork fabric, lining fabric, and fusible web, and cut out all the pieces neatly. Cut a main wallet piece measuring 6½ x 4½ in. (17 x 11 cm) from cork fabric, lining fabric, and fusible web.

TIP

Cork fabrics can be quite absorbent, so if you are using erasable fabric pens to transfer the motif, be sure to test on a scrap of material first to check that your marks don't bleed and can be easily removed.

2 Transfer the motif on page 81 onto the front half of the cork main wallet piece. Following the stitch guide, work the design in the corresponding colors and stitches.

TIP

Because cork fabric is comprised of two layers—a thin sheet of cork secured onto a woven backing—it has quite a solid structure. You may find that it is easier to hold it as you stitch rather than to secure it in a hoop. Experiment and see what works best for you!

3 Once the design is complete, place the embroidered cork wrong side up, with the fusible web on top and lining piece right side up on top of that. Cover with a pressing cloth or non-stick baking parchment. Following the manufacturer's instructions, fuse the layers together. Set aside.

4 Place the two cork wallet inserts wrong side up, with the fusible web on top and the corresponding lining pieces right side up on top of that. Cover with a pressing cloth or non-stick baking parchment. Following the manufacturer's instructions, fuse the layers together.

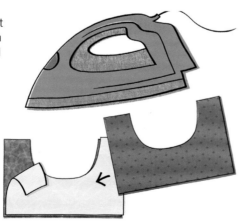

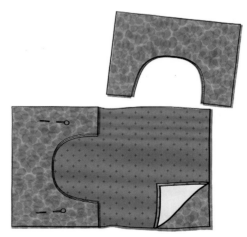

5 Place the main wallet piece lining side up, with a wallet insert at each end, cork side up, and pin together.

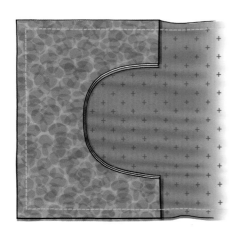

6 Stitch around the outer edge of the wallet by hand or by machine to secure the elements together, taking a ¼-in. (6-mm) seam allowance.

7 Fold the wallet in half where indicated on the pattern, cover with a pressing cloth, and press from the back to finish.

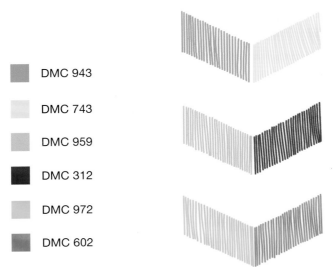

■	DMC 943
■	DMC 743
■	DMC 959
■	DMC 312
■	DMC 972
■	DMC 602

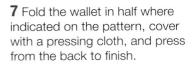 Satin stitch

drawstring bag

Drawstring bags are pretty yet practical projects. They make a great alternative to wrapping for a special gift, or are perfect for stowing away separate items when you pack your luggage. This simple drawstring bag has been accented with a geometric panel.

YOU WILL NEED

Low-volume cotton fabric, 15 x 12 in. (38 x 30 cm)

Polka-dot cotton fabric, 8 x 10½ in. (20 x 27 cm)

Plain cotton fabric for lining, 23 x 10½ in. (58.5 x 27 cm)

Striped cotton fabric for casing strip, 4½ x 8 in. (11.5 x 20 cm)

Embroidery flosses (threads)—one skein of each, all six strands used—in the following shades:
    Anchor 52 (Mid Rose)
    Anchor 241 (Forest Green)
    Anchor 298 (Deep Canary)
    Anchor 1070 (Very Light Aquamarine)
    Anchor 1090 (Light Bright Turquoise)

Cord, 32 in. (80 cm)

Wooden beads x 4

Motif and stitch guide on page 85

Fabric scissors, pinking shears, and embroidery scissors

Embroidery hoop, 5 in. (12.5 cm)

Embroidery needle

Thread conditioner (optional)

Sewing machine

Pins

Pressing cloth and iron

FINISHED MEASUREMENTS

8 x 10 in. (20 x 25 cm)

EMBROIDERY STITCHES USED

Satin stitch (see page 115)
Straight stitch (see page 116)

NOTE

The term "low-volume fabric" has been coined by the modern quilting movement and usually refers to a white, cream, or very light gray fabric with a subtle print—including dots, stripes, geometrics, and even text. These are often used as secondary fabrics to a design, where you want a different element—here, the hand embroidery—to stand out but don't want something as stark as a solid white cotton.

1 From the low-volume cotton, cut two 7¼ x 8½-in. (18.5 x 22-cm) pieces; these will form the outer bag. From the polka-dot cotton, cut two 3¾ x 8½-in. (9.5 x 22-cm) pieces for the contrast panels. From the lining fabric, cut two 8½ x 10¼-in. (22 x 26-cm) pieces. Set the polka-dot and lining pieces aside and work on one of the outer bag pieces.

2 Transfer the geometric motif on page 85 onto the front panel of the bag (see page 117). Secure the fabric in the embroidery hoop (see page 118) to create a neat, taut stitching surface. Following the stitch guide, work the design in the corresponding colors and stitches, repositioning the hoop as needed.

3 Once the design is complete, remove from the fabric from the hoop and trim the thread ends neatly. Cover with a pressing cloth and press on the reverse.

4 With right sides together, aligning the raw edges, place one of the polka-dot panels on the lower edge of the embroidered panel. Pin in place. Machine stitch together, taking a ⅜-in. (1-cm) seam allowance. Repeat to make the second outer panel. Press the seams toward the polka-dot panels.

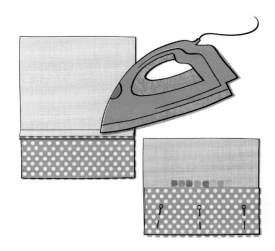

TIP

You can personalize this make
even more by adding your initials as
a stitched monogram, or even the
recipient's name if this is a gift.

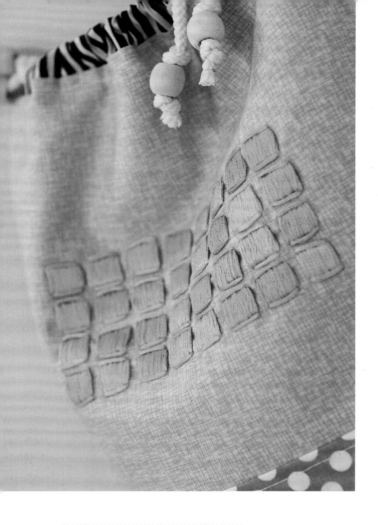

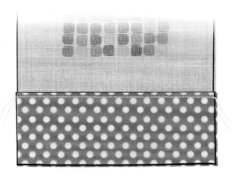

5 Work a line of neat machine topstitching across the top of the polka-dot panel to secure the seam allowance in place. Repeat on the second outer bag panel.

6 Along the upper edge of both outer bag pieces, fold ⅜ in. (1 cm) to the wrong side and press.

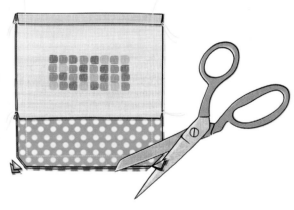

TIP

Pressing at each stage of the construction of the drawstring bag is the key to a really neat finish. Be sure to cover the embroidery with a pressing cloth so that the hot plate of the iron won't damage the delicate stitches.

7 Pin the two outer bag pieces right sides together. Machine stitch down the sides and across the bottom of the bag, taking a ⅜-in. (1-cm) seam allowance. Clip the seam allowances at the corners. Press.

8 Repeat steps 6 and 7 with the lining pieces.

9 Turn the outer bag right side out. With wrong sides together, aligning the seams, slide the lining inside the bag and pin along the upper folded sections.

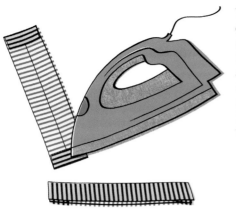

10 Cut the casing strip in half to give two 4½ x 4-in. (11.5 x 10-cm) pieces. Press each strip in half lengthways. Open out the strips again and, at each short end of each strip, press ⅜ in. (1 cm) to the wrong side. Fold along the center crease line again and machine stitch along the long unfolded edge to secure.

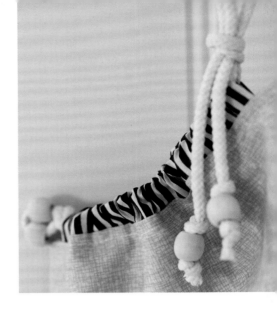

11 Slide the folded casing strip in between the outer bag and the lining, so that the raw edges are sandwiched in between, and pin in place. Topstitch in place.

TIP

If your sewing machine has a removable free arm, you may find it easier to work this upper seam with the arm removed.

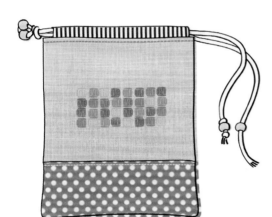

12 Thread two wooden beads onto the cord and slide them to the center before knotting them in place. Thread one end of the cord through the front casing and the other through the back casing. Thread a wooden bead onto each free end of the cord and knot to secure.

▢ ANC 298	
▢ ANC 52	
▢ ANC 1090	
▢ ANC 241	
▢ ANC 1070	

‖‖‖ Satin stitch

= Straight stitch

pocket mirror

Add a little personality to your cosmetics purse with a sweet woodland character motif. This design is stitched on a small piece of fabric before being secured in a pocket compact mirror. You can find all kind of fun blanks, from mirrors to keyfobs, in craft stores and online; they're great for displaying mini works like this.

YOU WILL NEED

Linen blend fabric (55% linen, 45% cotton) in a neutral color, 5-in. (12.5-cm) square

Embroidery flosses (threads)—one skein of each, all six strands used—in the following shades:
  DMC Blanco (white)
  DMC 310 (Black)
  DMC 900 (Dark Burnt Orange)

Motif and stitch guide on page 87

Oval mirror blank, 3 x 2½ in. (7.5 x 6 cm)

Fabric scissors, pinking shears, and embroidery scissors

Embroidery hoop, 4 in. (10 cm)

Embroidery needle

Thread conditioner (optional)

Sewing needle and cotton thread

High-tack glue

FINISHED MEASUREMENTS

Mirror blank: 3 x 2.5 in. (7.5 x 6 cm)
Embroidery: approx. 2¾ x 2 in. (7 x 5.5 cm)

EMBROIDERY STITCHES USED

Backstitch (see page 112)
French knots (see page 114)
Satin stitch (see page 115)

1 Using the pinking shears, trim the raw edges of the linen blend fabric to prevent it from fraying. Secure it in the embroidery hoop (see page 118) to create a neat, taut stitching surface.

2 Transfer the fox motif below onto the linen (see page 117), being sure to check that the design will fit neatly into the frame of the mirror blank. Following the stitch guide, work the design in the corresponding colors and stitches.

3 Once the fox character is complete, remove the fabric from the hoop and place it on the inner part of the mirror blank, ensuring that the motif is positioned as desired.

TIP

When gathering the fabric around the inner portion of the mirror blank you may need to work two rounds of gathering stitches to create a taut finish; alternatively, work ladder stitching (see page 54) across to secure the fabric in place.

4 Work a line of gathering stitches (see page 15) around the outer edge of the linen, using the sewing needle and cotton thread. Draw the thread up tightly to pull the excess fabric neatly around the inner part of the mirror blank, and knot to secure.

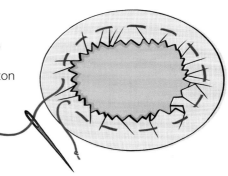

5 Apply a small amount of high-tack glue around the back of the work, and press it securely into the mirror blank to finish.

TIP

Pocket mirror blanks come in all different shapes, sizes, and styles. The construction principles are very similar, but some have an additional part that fits over the front of the design. Work with lightweight fabrics — otherwise, once the fabric is gathered, it may be too bulky for you to be able to clip all the parts of the mirror together.

DMC 900

DMC BLANCO

DMC 310

✎ Backstitch

o French knots

▮▮▮ Satin stitch

chapter 4

TO WEAR

flying high brooch

Paper planes remind us of childhood games and the simple folded shape of the airplane makes a striking doodle-style design to work in embroidery. Brooch blanks are a fantastic way to finish mini embroidery makes and to show off your stitches in true style.

YOU WILL NEED

Blue cotton chambray, 7-in. (18-cm) square

Embroidery flosses (threads)—one skein of each, all six strands used—in the following shades:
Anchor 2 (White)
Anchor 401 (Very Light Ash Gray)
Anchor 430 (Black)

Brooch blank, 1¾ in. (4.5 cm) in diameter

Motif and stitch guide on page 92

Fabric scissors, pinking shears, and embroidery scissors

Embroidery hoop, 4 in. (10 cm)

Embroidery needle

Thread conditioner (optional)

Pencil or tailor's chalk

Fray Check

Sewing needle and cotton thread

FINISHED MEASUREMENTS

1¾ in. (4.5 cm) in diameter

EMBROIDERY STITCHES USED

Running stitch (see page 115)
Satin stitch (see page 115)
Straight stitch (see page 115)

1 Using the pinking shears, trim the raw edges of the chambray to prevent it from fraying. Secure it in the embroidery hoop (see page 118) to create a neat, taut stitching surface.

2 Transfer the airplane motif on page 92 centrally onto the fabric (see page 117). Following the stitch guide, work the design in the corresponding colors and stitches.

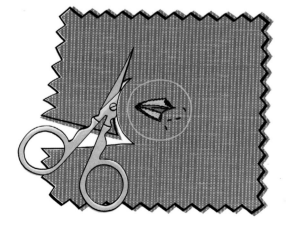

3 Once the design is complete, remove it from the hoop. Center the brooch blank on top of the embroidery and draw around it with a pencil or tailor's chalk. Trim the chambray to ¾ in. (2 cm) larger than the marking for the blank. This will create a 2½-in. (6.5-cm) circle with the embroidered design in the center.

TIP

Brooch blanks are usually made up of three parts: the outer section, which makes the frame; the inner part, around which the embroidery/fabric is secured; and the back, which covers the back of the work and features the brooch pin.

4 Following the manufacturer's instructions, apply a small amount of Fray Check to the edges to help bond the fibers and allow to dry.

5 Center the inner part of the brooch blank on the wrong side of the design. Using a sewing needle and thread, work a line of gathering stitches around the outer edge (see page 15). Draw up the thread to pull the fabric neatly around the brooch blank and secure firmly with a knot.

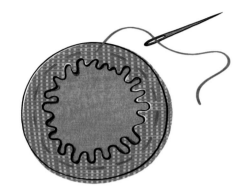

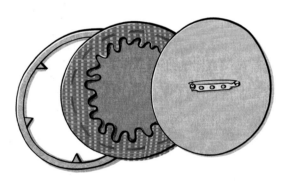

6 Following the manufacturer's instructions, sandwich the embroidery-covered inner section between the outer frame of the brooch and the back and secure it in place.

■	ANC 430
□	ANC 2
▨	ANC 401

- ⫶ Running stitch

- ⩘ Satin stitch

- ╱ Straight stitch

The white "wings" are also worked in satin stitch.

feeling fruity

Updating a garment can be as simple as adding a few new buttons, so why not create a whole set of fun, hand-stitched designs? Embroider these fruity motifs to transform plain coats or to give as gifts.

1 Using the pinking shears, trim the raw edges of the white cotton fabric to prevent it from fraying. Secure it in the embroidery hoop (see page 118) to create a neat, taut stitching surface.

2 Using the self-cover button template and the motifs on page 94, transfer the cover button shape and the fruit designs onto the fabric (see page 117), allowing some space between them. Following the stitch guide, work the designs in the corresponding colors and stitches.

3 Once the designs are complete, remove them from the hoop and cut out each of the round button shapes in turn.

4 Following the manufacturer's instructions, apply a small amount of Fray Check to the edges to help bond the fibers and allow to dry (see Tip, page 92).

TIP

You can use print fabrics as a base for your buttons, or scraps of plain fabric from your stash; just be sure that they are big enough to be held taut in a small hoop while you stitch.

YOU WILL NEED

White cotton fabric, 7 in. (17 cm) square

Embroidery flosses (threads)—one skein of each, all six strands used—in the following shades:

For the watermelon
DMC 326 (Very Dark Rose)
DMC 632 (Very Dark Desert Sand)
DMC 3011 (Dark Khaki Green)

For the peach
DMC 632 (Very Dark Desert Sand)
DMC 950 (Light Desert Sand)

For the pineapple
DMC 743 (Mid Yellow)
DMC 3011 (Dark Khaki Green)

Self-cover button kit and tool—1⅛-in. (2.9-cm) buttons

Motifs and stitch guide on page 94

Fabric scissors, pinking shears, and embroidery scissors

Embroidery hoop, 4½ in. (11 cm)

Embroidery needle

Thread conditioner (optional)

Fray Check

FINISHED MEASUREMENTS

Each button: 1⅛ in. (2.9 cm) in diameter

EMBROIDERY STITCHES USED

Backstitch (see page 112)
Satin stitch (see page 115)
Straight stitch (see page 116)

NOTE

Self-cover buttons come in a kit which includes a template for making up.

5 Working on each button in turn, place the embroidered fabric over the button front and work around the outer edge to secure the fabric in place.

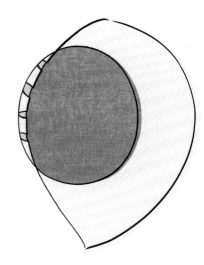

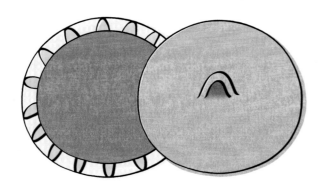

6 Make sure there are no creases in the fabric, then push the back of the button securely in place, covering all the raw edges of the fabric.

 DMC 950

DMC 632

DMC 326

 DMC 3011

DMC 743

 Backstitch

 Straight stitch

 Satin stitch

sew-on gems

Customize bags, clothing, or accessories with your own sew-on patches. They're worked in simple satin stitch and backstitch to create bold gem motifs that will add a touch of sparkle to any occasion.

YOU WILL NEED

White felt, 6-in. (15-cm) square (this is enough for both patches)

Dark gray felt, 6-in. (15-cm) square (this is enough for both patches)

Embroidery flosses (threads)—one skein of each, all six strands used—in the following shades:

For the emerald
DMC 164 (Light Forest Green)
DMC 562 (Mid Jade)
DMC 3813 (Light Blue Green)

For the ruby
DMC 350 (Mid Coral)
DMC 352 (Light Coral)
DMC 666 (Bright Red)

To outline each motif
DMC 310 (Black)

Motifs and stitch guide on page 97

Fabric and embroidery scissors

Embroidery hoop, 4 in. (10 cm)

Embroidery needle

Thread conditioner (optional)

High-tack glue

FINISHED MEASUREMENTS
Ruby: 2½ x 2½ in. (6 x 6 cm)
Emerald: 2 x 2¾ in. (5 x 7 cm)

EMBROIDERY STITCHES USED
Backstitch (see page 112)
Satin stitch (see page 115)

1 Secure the white felt in the embroidery hoop (see page 118) to create a neat, taut stitching surface.

2 Transfer the ruby and emerald motifs on page 126 onto the felt (see page 117), leaving a border of at least ¾ in. (2 cm) around each one. Following the stitch guide, work the designs in the corresponding colors and stitches.

TIP

Keeping the felt taut will help you to make neat, even stitches. Be aware that, if you need to remove the stitches to make corrections, the needle holes can remain visible in felt.

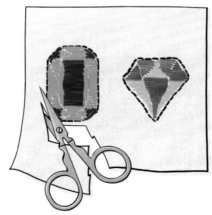

3 Once the designs are complete, remove the felt from the hoop and neatly trim to leave a ¼-in. (6-mm) border around each motif.

4 Place the embroidered gems on the dark gray felt and secure with a few small dabs of high-tack glue. Backstitch around each one using black embroidery floss (thread).

5 To finish, neatly cut around the motifs to leave a ¼-in. (6-mm) gray felt border around each one.

TIP

These gems can be custom made in any color you like. Try working with a palette of ombré shades to give a more realistic finish.

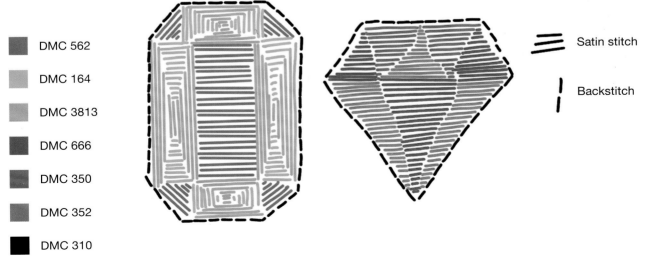

▪	DMC 562
▪	DMC 164
▪	DMC 3813
▪	DMC 666
▪	DMC 350
▪	DMC 352
▪	DMC 310

≡ Satin stitch

❘ Backstitch

customized cardigan

Give a cozy but plain cardi a fresh look by adding an embroidered motif. This woodland-inspired design is the perfect match for those chilly autumnal days.

YOU WILL NEED

Cardigan

Embroidery flosses (threads)—one skein of each, all six strands used—in the following shades:
  Anchor 338 (Light Terracotta)
  Anchor 379 (Mid Mocha Beige)
  Anchor 956 (Very Light Drab Brown)
  Anchor 1025 (Very Dark Salmon)
  Anchor 5975 (Terracotta)

Motif and stitch guide on page 99

Embroidery hoop, 6 in. (15 cm)

Embroidery needle

Embroidery scissors

Thread conditioner (optional)

Pressing cloth and iron

FINISHED MEASUREMENTS
Autumnal motif: 4 x 2¾ in. (10 x 7 cm)

EMBROIDERY STITCHES USED
Backstitch (see page 112)
French knots (see page 114)
Satin stitch (see page 115)
Straight stitch (see page 116)

1 Place the cardigan in the hoop so that the section where you want the embroidery to go is held under even tension (see page 118).

2 Transfer the autumnal motif on page 99 onto the cardigan (see page 117). Following the stitch guide, work the design in the corresponding colors and stitches.

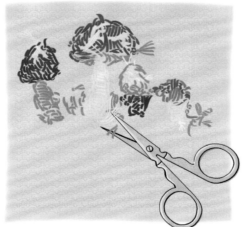

3 Once the design is complete, remove the cardigan from the hoop and neatly trim all the thread ends.

TIP

Knitted fabrics are very stretchy, so be sure to secure the cardigan in the hoop so that it is under an even tension; the stitches of the knitted fabric should be neither too stretched nor too baggy. An even tension will help you to create a neat embroidered motif.

4 Cover the back of the embroidery with a pressing cloth or soft towel and press to finish.

TIP

Although many brands of embroidery floss (thread) are described as being color fast, it is always advisable to hand wash customized garments such as this, as this will help to prevent any color runs and also increase the longevity of the garment.

ANC 1025	
ANC 5975	
ANC 338	
ANC 379	
ANC 956	

O French knot

/ Straight stitch

/// Satin stitch

| Backstitch

Handmade jewelry and accessories are true statement pieces and guaranteed to become a talking point for anyone who sees them. Worked in a selection of jewel-toned threads, this feather motif is crafted into a fabric cuff, allowing you to accessorize with your embroidered stitches.

feathered fancy

YOU WILL NEED

Lilac cotton fabric, 8 in. (20 cm) square

Felt, 6½ x 2½ in. (16.5 x 6.5 cm)

Heavyweight fusible interfacing, 6½ x 2½ in. (16.5 x 6.5 cm)

Embroidery flosses (threads)—one skein of each, all six strands used—in the following shades:
  DMC 350 (Mid Coral)
  DMC 518 (Light Wedgwood Blue)
  DMC 552 (Mid Violet)
  DMC 741 (Mid Tangerine)
  DMC 959 (Mid Seagreen)
  DMC 962 (Mid Dusty Rose)
  DMC 3041 (Mid Antique Violet)

Button, ¾ in. (2 cm) long

Motif and stitch guide on page 101

Fabric scissors, pinking shears, and embroidery scissors

Embroidery hoop, 6 in. (15 cm)

Embroidery needle

Thread conditioner (optional)

Pins

Sewing needle and cotton thread

Pressing cloth and iron

FINISHED MEASUREMENTS

6½ x 2½ in. (16.5 x 6.5 cm), with a 1½-in (4-cm) buttonhole loop

EMBROIDERY STITCHES USED

Backstitch (see page 112)
Blanket stitch (see page 112)
Buttonhole stitch (see page 113)
Couching (see page 113)
French knots (see page 114)
Straight stitch (see page 116)

1 Using the pinking shears, trim the raw edges of the cotton fabric to prevent it from fraying. Secure it in the embroidery hoop (see page 118) to create a neat, taut stitching surface.

2 Transfer the feather motif on page 101 centrally onto the fabric (see page 117). Following the stitch guide, work the design in the corresponding colors and stitches.

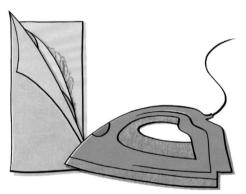

TIP

Using a pressing cloth against the embroidered stitches will prevent them from getting damaged or crushed when the iron is used to apply the interfacing.

3 Once the embroidery is complete, remove it from the hoop and trim it 7 x 3 in. (18 x 7.5 cm). Trim the interfacing to 6½ x 2½ in. (16.5 x 6.5 cm) and center it on the back of the embroidery. Cover with a pressing cloth and fuse in position, following the manufacturer's instructions.

4 Fold ¼ in. (5 mm) of lilac cotton to the wrong side over the interfacing and finger press it in place. Place the strip of felt over the back of the interfacing and pin it in place. Using blanket stitch, work around the edge of the cuff to secure the cotton upper to the felt backing.

5 Center the button on one short end of the cuff and stitch it in place, using the sewing needle and doubled cotton thread.

6 With a length of embroidery thread, work four ¾-in. (2-cm) loops on the opposite end of the cuff to the button. If you need to make the cuff larger or smaller, simply measure it against your wrist and increase or decrease the size of the loops as required. Holding all the loops together as one, work around them with buttonhole loop stitches to secure.

TIP

Check the length of the cuff against your wrist as you work the foundation of the buttonhole loops to make sure the cuff is the right size for you.

DMC 518

DMC 741

DMC 962

DMC 959

DMC 350

DMC 552

DMC 3041

/ Backstitch

∿ Straight stitch worked in zig zag pattern

0 French knot

Couching

| Straight stitch

statement necklace

Geometric patterns are great foundations for dramatic designs. These repeated triangles are worked in satin stitch in bold modern shades for a really stand-out finish.

YOU WILL NEED

White felt, 8-in. (20-cm) square

Dark gray felt, 8-in. (20-cm) square

Embroidery flosses (threads)—one skein of each, all six strands used—in the following shades:
  Anchor 214 (Light Pistachio Green)
  Anchor 279 (Light Olive Green)
  Anchor 328 (Apricot)
  Anchor 877 (Dark Celadon Green)
  Anchor 920 (Light Antique Blue)
  Anchor 1064 (Turquoise)
  Anchor 1096 (Very Light Antique Blue)

Grosgrain ribbon, 60 in. (150 cm), ⅝ in. (1.5 cm) wide

Two 5-mm jump rings

Motif and stitch guide on page 104

Fabric and embroidery scissors

Embroidery hoop, 6 in. (15 cm)

Embroidery needle

Thread conditioner (optional)

High-tack glue

Sewing needle and cotton thread

FINISHED MEASUREMENTS

5¾ x 2½ in. (14.5 x 6 cm)

EMBROIDERY STITCHES USED

Backstitch (see page 112)
Satin stitch (see page 115)

1 Secure the white felt in the embroidery hoop (see page 118) to create a neat, taut stitching surface.

2 Transfer the geometric motif on page 126 onto the felt (see page 117). Following the stitch guide, work the design in the corresponding colors and stitches.

TIP

Felt is a great material to work with, as it won't fray after it's been cut, but be aware that it can stretch out of shape if it's held under too much tension.

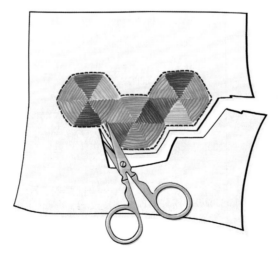

3 Once the design is complete, remove it from the hoop and neatly cut around the motif, leaving a ¼-in. (6-mm) border all around.

4 Place the embroidered panel on the dark gray felt and secure with a few small dabs of high-tack glue.

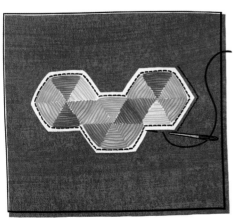

5 Secure the motif to the gray felt by backstitching around it in black embroidery floss (thread).

6 Neatly trim the dark gray felt, leaving a ¼-in. (6-mm) border around the motif.

7 Working on each side in turn, position a jump ring at the upper section on the back of the gray felt and secure with a few hand stitches, using the sewing needle and cotton thread.

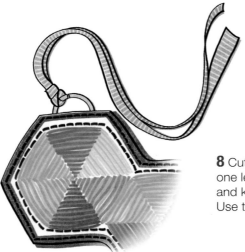

8 Cut the grosgrain ribbon in half lengthwise. Fold one length in half again, feed it through a jump ring, and knot to secure. Repeat on the second side. Use the ribbons ends to tie the necklace.

ANC 328

ANC 279

ANC 214

ANC 1096

ANC 877

ANC 1064

ANC 920

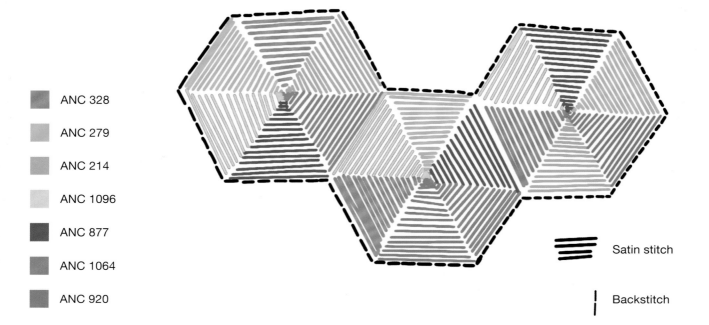

Satin stitch

Backstitch

YOU WILL NEED

Linen blend fabric (55% linen, 45% cotton) in a neutral color, one 6-in. (15-cm) and two 3-in. (8-cm) squares

For the necklace

Embroidery flosses (threads)—one skein of each, all six strands used unless otherwise stated—in the following shades:
  Anchor 9 (Light Coral)
  Anchor 96 (Light Violet)
  Anchor 379 (Mid Mocha Beige)—
    use three strands only
  Anchor 831 (Very Light Drab Brown)
  Anchor 1092 (Light Seagreen)

Miniature oval embroidery hoop, 2½ x 1⅜-in. (6.2 x 3.4-cm)

16-in. (40-cm) chain necklace

1 x 5mm jump ring

For the earrings

Embroidery flosses (threads)—one skein of each, all six strands used—in the following shades:
  Anchor 9 (Light Coral)
  Anchor 96 (Light Violet)
  Anchor 128 (Very Light Baby Blue)
  Anchor 214 (Light Pistachio Green)
  Anchor 1092 (Light Seagreen)
  Anchor 1094 (Very Light Cranberry)

Miniature round embroidery hoops, 2 x 1½-in. (4-cm)

2 x earwire findings

2 x 5mm jump rings

For the necklace and earrings

Motifs and stitch guide on page 107

Fabric scissors, pinking shears, and embroidery scissors

Embroidery hoop, 4½ in. (11 cm)

Embroidery needle

Thread conditioner (optional)

Jewelry pliers (optional)

High-tack glue

Sewing needle and cotton thread

FINISHED MEASUREMENTS

Necklace: 2½ x 1⅜ in. (6.2 x 3.4 cm)
Earrings: 1½ in. (4 cm) in diameter

EMBROIDERY STITCHES USED

French knots (see page 114)
Stem stitch (see page 115)
Straight stitch (see page 116)

Miniature designs can really pack a punch when added to striking scaled-down frames. These confectionery-inspired designs are made into a necklace and earring set that looks good enough to eat!

ice cream necklace and sprinkles earring set

MAKING THE NECKLACE

1 First, make the necklace. Using the pinking shears, trim the raw edges of the large piece of linen fabric to prevent it from fraying. Secure it in the embroidery hoop (see page 118) to create a neat, taut stitching surface.

2 Transfer the ice-cream motif on page 107 centrally onto the fabric (see page 117), making sure it fits within the inner aperture of the miniature hoop. Following the stitch guide, work the design in the corresponding colors and stitches.

TIP

Mark out the inner aperture of the frame on your fabrics to ensure that the motif will fit within the frame.

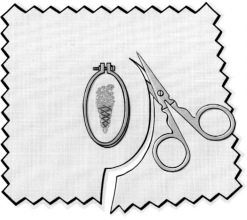

3 Once the design is complete, remove it from the embroidery hoop and position it centrally in the miniature hoop. Draw around the frame with tailor's chalk, then trim the fabric to ⅜ in. (1 cm) larger all around than the frame and position it in the frame.

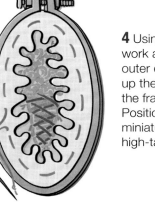

4 Using a sewing needle and cotton thread, work a line of gathering stitches around the outer edge of the fabric (see page 15). Draw up the thread to pull the fabric neatly around the frame and knot the threads to secure. Position the backing element of the miniature frame in place and secure with high-tack glue.

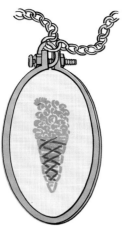

5 Attach the jump ring to the bolt on the miniature frame (you may need to use pliers to open the ring), then feed the chain through the jump ring to finish the necklace.

TIP

Necklace chains and earring fastenings can be found in the jewelry findings section of craft stores or at specialist stores. Take the finished embroideries mounted in the frames to the store to help you select the findings.

MAKING THE EARRINGS

1 Repeat steps 1-4 of the necklace to make the sprinkles earring hoops.

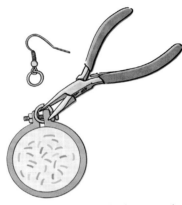

2 Attach a jump ring to the bolt on each miniature frame (you may need to use pliers to open the rings), then attach the earwire findings to the jump rings.

![ANC 96]	ANC 96
![ANC 1092]	ANC 1092
![ANC 9]	ANC 9
![ANC 831]	ANC 831
![ANC 379]	ANC 379
![ANC 214]	ANC 214
![ANC 1094]	ANC 1094
![ANC 128]	ANC 128

O   French knot

≡   Satin stitch

Straight stitch

embroidered button-down shirt

The button-down shirt is a closet staple, but that doesn't mean it has to be boring. Add a unique touch with a custom embroidery—this bright flamingo design is sure to turn heads!

YOU WILL NEED

Button-down shirt

Embroidery flosses (threads)—one skein of each, only three strands used unless otherwise stated—in the following shades:
  Anchor 2 (White)
  Anchor 60 (Mid Mauve)
  Anchor 62 (Cranberry)
  Anchor 328 (Apricot)—use all six strands when working the flamingo legs
  Anchor 403 (Black)
  Anchor 1094 (Very Light Cranberry)

Motif and stitch guide on page 109

Embroidery hoop, 5 in. (12 cm)

Embroidery needle

Embroidery scissors

Thread conditioner (optional)

Pressing cloth and iron

FINISHED MEASUREMENTS

Flamingo motif: approx. 4 x 2¾ in. (10 x 7 cm)

EMBROIDERY STITCHES USED

French knot (see page 114)
Long and short stitch—worked at random (see page 115)
Satin stitch (see page 115)
Stem stitch (see page 115)

1 Place the shirt in the hoop so that the section where you want the embroidery to go is held under even tension (see page 118).

2 Transfer the flamingo motif on page 109 onto the fabric (see page 117). Following the stitch guide, work the design in the corresponding colors and stitches.

TIP

Working the long and short stitches at random creates a more organic look and a feather-like texture.

3 Once the design is stitched, ensure that all the thread ends are neatly knotted and trimmed.

4 Remove from the hoop, place a pressing cloth or soft towel over the back of the embroidery, and press (see page 119).

 ANC 328

ANC 62

ANC 1094

ANC 60

ANC 403

ANC 2

O   French knot

///   Long and short stitch worked at random

∫   Stem stitch

||| Satin stitch

Breathe fresh life into a classic denim jacket and add a pop of color to your closet. This nautical motif was inspired by traditional sailor tattoos. You can maximize the effect by repeating the design—or elements of it—on the front of the jacket, too!

denim jacket

YOU WILL NEED

Denim jacket or other garment for customizing

Embroidery flosses (threads)—one skein of each, all six strands used—in the following shades:
Anchor 46 (Bright Red)
Anchor 291 (Dark Lemon)
Anchor 403 (Black)
Anchor 977 (Mid Baby Blue)

Motif and stitch guide on page 111

Embroidery hoop, 5 in. (12.5 cm)

Embroidery needle

Embroidery scissors

Thread conditioner (optional)

Thimble (optional)

Pressing cloth and iron

FINISHED MEASUREMENTS

Anchor motif: approx. 2½ x 3 in. (6 x 7.5 cm)

EMBROIDERY STITCHES USED

Backstitch (see page 112)
Chain stitch (see page 113)
French knots (see page 114)
Satin stitch (see page 115)
Straight stitch stars (see page 116)

1 Transfer the anchor motif onto the back of the denim jacket (see page 118). Position the hoop to work on one element of the design (see page 117).

TIP

Denim is a heavy fabric and—especially if the garment has two layers—it can be tough to stitch through. Use a thimble to protect your fingertips and a thread conditioner or beeswax to help the threads glide through the fabric.

2 Following the stitch guide, work the design in the corresponding colors and stitches.

TIP

Because the motif is worked across the upper back panel of the jacket, it is easier to use a small hoop and work on small sections at a time. After you have completed one section, simply remove the hoop and reposition it before working the next.

3 Once each section is complete, reposition the hoop and stitch the next area. Once the design is complete, fasten off and trim the threads neatly. Place the jacket under a pressing cloth and press the reverse to finish.

This chart is reproduced at 50%.
To make it full size, you will need to
enlarge it by 200% on a photocopier.

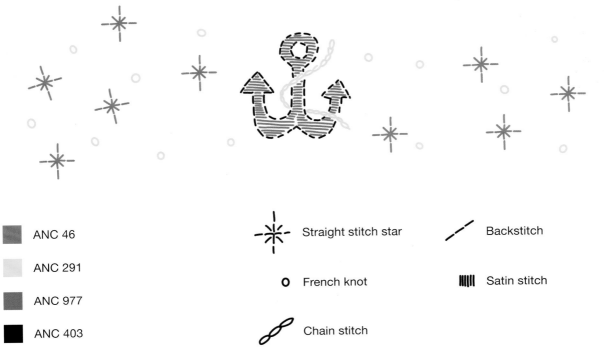

ANC 46

ANC 291

ANC 977

ANC 403

Straight stitch star

French knot

Chain stitch

Backstitch

Satin stitch

techniques

Embroidery stitches

There are literally hundreds of different embroidery stitches! These are the ones I've used in this book, but feel free to experiment and substitute other stitches for the ones I've suggested if you prefer. All the projects use stranded embroidery floss and, in most cases,

I've used all six strands; however, if you're using a fine, lightweight fabric, you might prefer to use fewer strands for a more delicate look. Before you start a project, work a few stitches on a piece of scrap fabric to see if you like the effect.

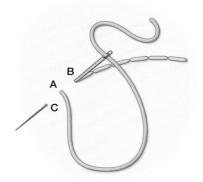

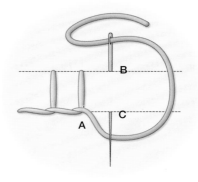

Backstitch
Bring the needle up at A, take it back down one stitch length behind this point at B, and bring it up again at C, one stitch length in front of the point at which it first emerged. Repeat as required.

Blanket stitch
Bring the needle up at the edge of the fabric at A. Insert the needle at B, to the right and above the edge, and take it back down at C, looping the floss (thread) under the tip of the needle. Pull through to secure.

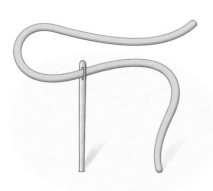

Bullion stitch

1 Bring the needle up, then take it back down a stitch length to the left. Draw the needle through, leaving a loop of floss (thread) on the surface of the fabric.

2 Bring the needle back up close to the point at which it first emerged, then wrap the loop of floss around the tip of the needle five times.

3 Take the needle back down at the second entry point and pull through to secure.

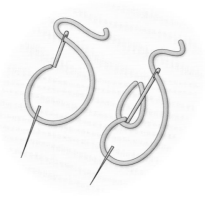

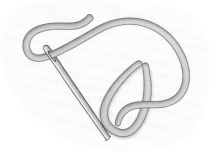

Buttonhole stitch

Work as for blanket stitch (see page 112), keeping the stitches very close together so that no fabric is visible in between.

Chain stitch

Bring the needle up on the surface of the fabric. Take it back down next to the point at which it emerged and bring back up directly below to create the start of the next stitch, looping the floss (thread) under the tip of the needle. Draw up to tighten the loop on the surface of the fabric. To make the next stitch in the chain, insert the needle next to the point at which the floss emerged and bring it out a stitch length away, again looping the floss under the needle tip.

Lazy daisy (also known as detached chain stitch)

This is a variation on chain stitch and makes individual "chain links" that can be used to create "petals." When you've made the first loop, insert the needle over the loop of floss (thread) to hold the loop down.

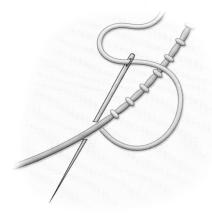

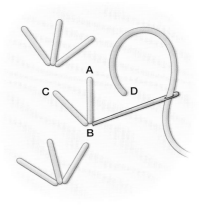

Couching

Couching is a technique for securing a length of floss (thread), cord, or yarn to the surface of the fabric. Bring the main floss to the surface of the fabric and lay it along the line you want it to follow. With a second length of floss, work evenly spaced straight stitches across the main floss to secure it to the fabric; these stitches are called "tie stitches."

Cross stitch

To work a line of cross stitches, work a series of diagonal stitches along the length of the line, then work back over them to complete the "crosses."

Fern stitch

Bring the needle to the surface of the fabric at A and take it down at B. Bring the needle back to the surface at C, to the left of the first stitch, and pass it back down through the fabric at B to make a V, then back up at D and down at B. This can be worked either as individual stitches (as shown), or in a row.

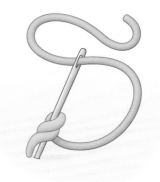

French knots
Bring the needle up to the surface at the position of the knot. Holding the floss (thread) taut, wrap it two or three times around the tip of the needle. Continue holding the floss under tension as you pass the needle back down through the fabric close to the entry point. The floss will pull through the wraps and they will form a knot that sits on the surface of the fabric.

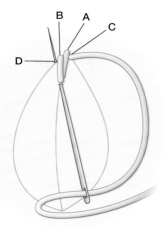

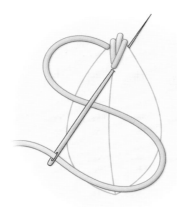

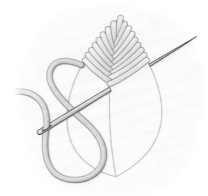

Herringbone leaf stitch

1 Work a straight stitch by bringing the needle to the surface at A, then back down directly below, on the center line. Bring the needle up to the surface at B (immediately to the left of A), then pass it back down on the center line and back up again at C (immediately to the right of A). Insert the needle on the center line again, below the previous stitches, and bring it out at D.

2 Repeat this process of inserting the needle on the center line and bringing it out alternately to the left and right of the leaf shape.

3 Keep adding the layers on each side around the leaf shape, making sure all the stitch points lie close together so that no fabric is visible in between.

Long and short stitch

Bring the needle to the surface and take it back down directly below, creating a long straight stitch. Bring the needle back up directly next to the first entry point and take it back down at the halfway point along the long stitch. This creates a long straight stitch followed by a short straight stitch; alternate these as needed.

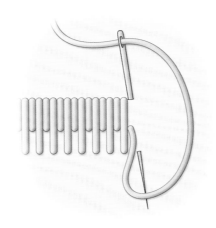

Running stitch

Bring the needle to the surface of the fabric and take it back down to the left of the entry point, to create a straight stitch. Bring the needle back to the surface a stitch length away from the last stitch and return through the fabric as before. Continue to create stitches of equal length.

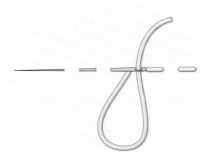

Long and short stitch worked at random

Work as long and short stitch, above left, but the stitches do not need to be worked in a neat line: long stitches and short stitches are worked in a random fashion as needed.

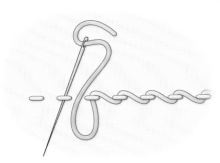

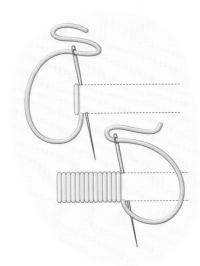

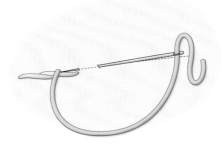

Threaded running stitch

Once a line of running stitch is completed, as above, bring a contrast floss (thread) to the surface at the start of a stitch, then pass the needle under the first running stitch without piercing the fabric. Continue along the length of running stitches, working up and down.

Satin stitch

Bring the needle up to the surface of the fabric, then take it back down at the selected point, drawing the floss (thread) flush against the fabric. Bring the needle back up and down again next to the previous stitch. Continue in this manner, drawing the floss smoothly against the surface of the fabric to fill the chosen area. The stitches should be close together, with no fabric visible in between them.

Stem stitch

Bring the needle up to the surface of the fabric and take it back down to create a straight stitch. Begin the second stitch by bringing the needle up to the surface partway along the first stitch, pushing the floss (thread) slightly to the side. Return the needle through the fabric to complete the stitch.

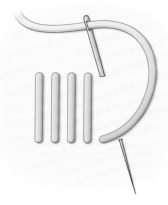

Straight stitch

Bring the needle through to the surface of the fabric and then take it back down to create a small straight stitch. These can be worked at random or as part of a design.

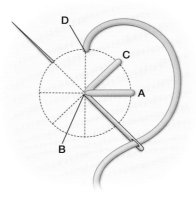

Straight stitch star

Start by drawing a circle on your fabric and marking the intervals at which the "points" of the star will sit. Work a horizontal straight stitch from point A to the center of the circle (B). Bring the needle up at point C and back down again at B, then bring the needle up at D and back down again at B. Continue to add straight stitches from the edge of the circle to the center (B), keeping all the stitches the same length and the same distance apart. You can also work half a star, as on the Stitch Sampler Pillow (page 62), or with elongated elements, as on the Denim Jacket (page 110).

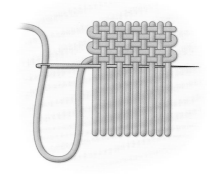

Weave stitch

With your main color, work a series of long straight stitches across the desired area. Using a contrast floss (thread) and working from left to right, bring the needle up at one side and weave it under and over the floss across the section, ending by passing the floss down through the work. Continue until the whole area is filled.

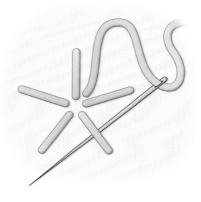

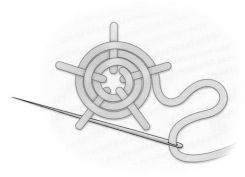

Woven rose

1 Create a foundation by working five straight stitches equidistant in toward a center point; this can be done in a contrast thread. Bring the needle to the surface of the fabric at the center of the stitches and begin working around the shape, passing the needle under one stitch and over the next.

2 Continue until the foundation straight stitches are covered, then take the needle to the back of the work and secure to finish.

Transferring motifs

There are a number of different ways that you can transfer a design onto fabric for embroidery. You may find that the design, style, color, weight of fabric, or your own preferences will dictate the method you use.

It's a good idea to familiarize yourself with the various techniques and different equipment required, so that you can use the best technique for each project you work on.

If you are working with a lightweight fabric in a light color, you may be able to trace the design directly onto the cloth. Place the cloth over the motif and use a transfer pencil or pen to mark the motif. You can also place the motif and fabric on a lightbox, or tape them to a window, and use the light source to help you plot the motif on the cloth.

Templates
It might be preferable to draw (or trace) the design onto paper, cut it out, and place it on your fabric to create a template. You will be able to draw around the design using your preferred transfer pen or pencil. This method is great for simple shapes and when fabric is very dark or heavy.

Needle punching
This is commonly used for paper or unusual fabrics. Pin the motif, or a tracing of the motif, to the surface of the fabric or paper and punch holes at regular intervals along the design with a sharp needle to provide a guide for the stitching.

Transfer paper
A specialist paper called transfer paper or dressmaker's carbon paper can be used when you want to position a design on a thick or dark fabric. Sandwich the paper between the fabric and the motif to be transferred, with the carbon surface facing the fabric. Work over the design using a knitting needle or similar with a steady pressure; the carbon paper will leave the outline of the design on the fabric.

Securing fabric in the hoop

Begin with a piece of cloth that is approximately 4 in. (10 cm) larger all round than the embroidery hoop you are using.

Using pinking shears, trim the raw edges of the fabric to prevent fraying

Open the hoop and position the lower section below the fabric and the upper section above centrally on the fabric, then carefully slide the two together.

Draw the edges of the fabric out evenly around the hoop to create a neat, taut stitching surface and tighten any screws on the hoop to secure.

TIP

If you find that your fabric is slipping out of the hoop or you are unable to maintain the tension across the fabric as you work, simply take the hoop apart and neatly wrap the inner hoop with a 1-in. (2.5-cm) wide strip of cotton fabric or bias tape. Once you've covered the inner hoop, replace the stitching fabric; the wrapped hoop should help to hold the fabric at the right tension.

Securing floss (thread)

When you start stitching, work a small knot at the end of the floss (thread) once the needle is threaded; this will secure it to the back of the work while you stitch. You can snip away any floss tails at the end to keep it neat.

Once you have worked your stitches and have finished a section or color, you will need to fasten off the floss to stop it from coming undone. To do this, simply end the stitch with the needle and floss on the back of the work, make a small stitch through the stitches on the back of the work, and fasten with a small neat knot and trim the floss ends neatly.

Pressing a completed embroidery

When you have finished stitching, you will often want to press your work—especially if it has been secured in a hoop that has left a circular crease in the fabric when it's removed. Place your embroidery on an ironing board, with the wrong side uppermost. Put a pressing cloth on top and press with an iron on a medium setting. A soft towel is a great choice for a pressing cloth, as the fluffy fibers protect the stitches.

When pressing, place the iron on the fabric and hold it there for a couple of seconds before lifting and repositioning—rather than using the sweeping motion that you would use to iron a wrinkled garment. By doing so you will be protecting the stitches and avoid warping them with the heat and motion of the iron.

All templates are full size unless instructed otherwise.

ABCDEFGHIJKLMNOPQRSTUVWXYZ&

12345
67890

This template is reproduced at 25% of the original size. You will need to enlarge it by 400%.

snowflake gift tag

pages 70-72

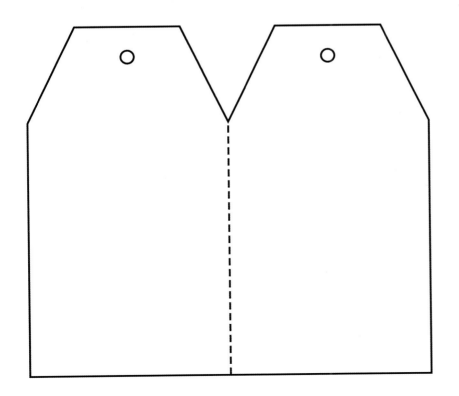

bumblebee purse
pages 76-78

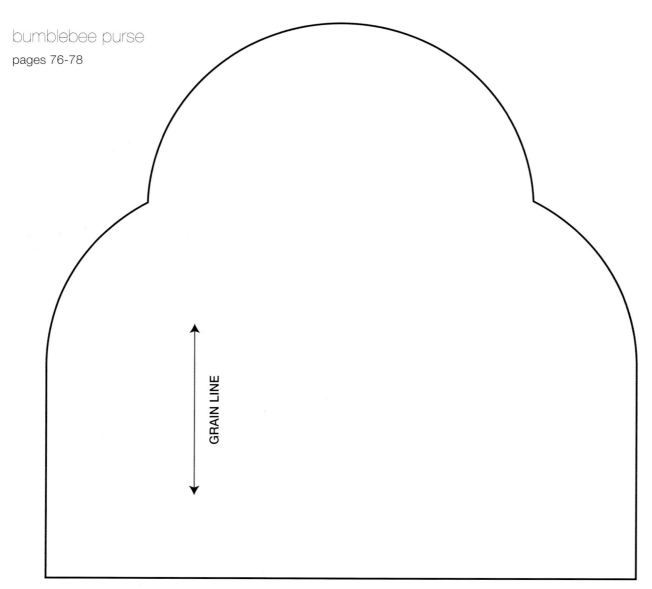

GRAIN LINE

MAIN

INSERTS

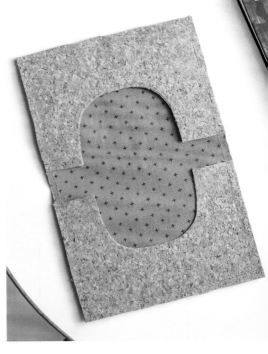

statement necklace

pages 102-104

sew-on gems

pages 96-97

suppliers

Anchor Threads
www.anchorcrafts.com

Cloud Craft
www.cloudcraft.co.uk

DMC
www.dmc.com

Hawthorn Handmade
www.hawthornhandmade.com

Hobbycraft
www.hobbycraft.co.uk

Joann
www.joann.com

John Lewis
www.johnlewis.com

Michaels
www.michaels.com

Sublime Stitching
www.sublimestitching.com

Vlieseline
www.vlieseline.com

acknowledgments

It has been a real pleasure to work on this collection of modern embroidery designs. The fabulous team of editors, designers, illustrators, and photographers has, as always, made a truly stunning book. I would like to extend special thanks to Cindy Richards, Penny Craig, Sally Powell, Sarah Hoggett, and the team at CICO.

It is an incredible privilege to work in such a creative career and I hope to always show my gratitude through hard work, motivation, and dedication to this creative sector. There is a phenomenal online community of stitchers, textile artists, and designers who are always a wealth of wisdom, support, and encouragement, many of whom are dear friends and also readers of www.madepeachy.com. I hope that you love this book as much as I loved making it—thank you!

Thank you to my brilliant family and friends, who are supportive of my every endeavor—whether they fully understand my obsession with textiles or not!

Finally, to John, my husband, and our sweet little family—thank you for joining me on this wonderful adventure!

index